I0500133

THE PHIZ ILLUSTRATIONS OF
DAVID COPPERFIELD

© George Valsamis, 2013

ELPENOR EDITIONS IN PRINT — www.elpenor.org

George Valsamis

The Phiz
Illustrations of Dickens'
David Copperfield

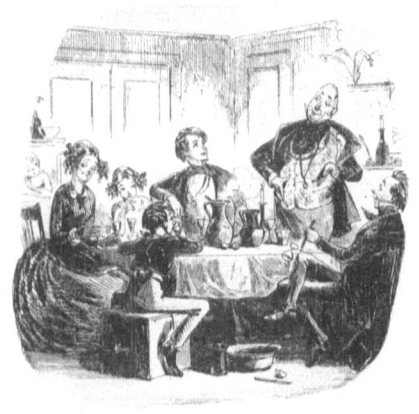

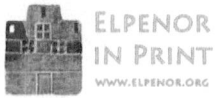

Athens 2013

Contents

Introduction

*T*he purpose of this book[1] is not to gather the original illustrations of David Copperfield, rather to follow them as they become a gate to the novel itself, this way fulfilling their own intention.

If you have read David Copperfield, this book will help you recall it, and if you haven't, the combination of the illustrations with chapter excerpts provides a great introduction to the power of Dickens' writing, the characters and the most important themes and developments, since Phiz co-operated with the author in what and how should be selected: this anthology is indeed a realization of what Dickens himself thought as crucial for a possible overview and presentation of his favorite novel.

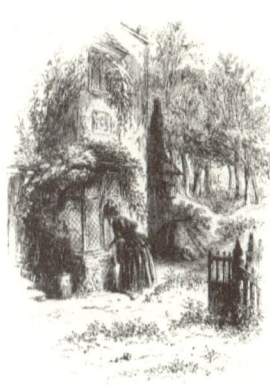

David's Aunt and Mr. Dick, Dora and Agnes, Steerforth and his mother, the Murdstones, Mr. Micawber and his family, Mrs. Gummidge, little Em'ly, Ham, the Pegottys and the Spenlows, Martha, Uriah Heep, the Doctor, Miss Mowcher, Mr. Barkis, Mr. Wickfield, Traddles..., all appear in this illustration-centered anthology, proving that Dickens co-operating with Phiz managed to provide a superb overview of the novel.

---

[1] A first form appeared on line at the David Copperfield web site — www.ellopos.net

In 1836 Hablot Knight Browne met and started working with the 25 years old Charles Dickens in the first of his novels, the Pickwick Papers, becoming a friend and his main illustrator since — in etching or in wood-engraving, in ten of fifteen novels, for 23 years. The illustrations for David Copperfield are the most famous together with those for Martin Chuzzlewit.

Valerie Browne Lester (Gresham Lecture, Nov. 28, 2006) describes the beginning of Dickens' friendship with Phiz as the foundation of a common development: "in the first years of their collaboration, they became constant companions, travelling all over the country together, even going abroad together, along with Dickens's wife, to recover from the death of her sister, Mary Hogarth. ... Dickens enjoyed Phiz's amiability and quiet humor; Phiz was drawn to Dickens's flash and dash. They even enjoyed playing battledore-and-shuttlecock together... As Dickens matured and deepened, so did he."

Chesterton (in Charles Dickens, 1906) describes their creative relationship as intense to a degree never surpassed by any other illustrator, "they were as suited to each other and to the common creation of a unique thing as Gilbert and Sullivan. No other illustrator ever created the true Dickens characters with the precise and correct quantum of exaggeration. No other illustrator ever breathed the true Dickens atmosphere, in which clerks are clerks and yet at the same time elves."

The 'Phiz' pseudonym was a means for the artist "to harmonize ... better with Dickens's Boz", according to himself, but Lester (*loc. cit.*) gives some more reasons:

"It happens that physiognomy was all the rage at the time; it is also true that the word 'phiz' is slang for face; and Dickens had just introduced a character called Fizkin into the novel. Phiz was definitely in the air."

*T*he initial monthly illustration for David Copper-field, *"Our Pew at Church"*, pictures an atmosphere of light-hearted sleepiness, introducing the happy days of David's childhood with his mother and his nurse Pegot-ty. The green color itself, the color of youth, life and joy, along with the welcoming protecting shady trees of the church pro-vide a context where even tombstones hide nothing frightening but a life of blessed quietness. The illustration focuses on the core of the society, the congregation, discerning lack of interest in faith, not atheism, but a consciousness that can be called 're-tired.' In this environment, the figure of Murdstone appears as if a characteristic product of a decadence. A neutral condition is impossible: absence of good provides already the presence of evil.

Not only the start but also the end of the novel comes in the beginning of time, in a joyful hour of a spring, when David and Agnes playing with their children by the fire receive Mr. Pegotty, an old man now yet vigorous, robust, and handsome, this way suggesting a fullness of happiness containing suffering, a pain that appears for the first time among these illustrations in *"I Make Myself Known To My Aunt"*.

"Changes At Home" already includes references to the trou-ble brought by the marriage of David's mother, yet even the fact of her being alive is enough to postpone real pain. As Da-vid admits, his heart was able still to become brim-full, so that recalling her singing to his newborn brother, although leading now himself a happy life with Agnes and his own children, makes him wishing he had died... *"I wish I had died then, with that feeling in my heart! I should have been more fit for Heaven than I ever have been since."*

"I Am Hospitably Received By Mr. Peggotty" (from chapter 3,

"I Have A Change") forms an impressive antithesis to the first illustration; both are based in the gothic arch, so that the warm and personal space in the boat-house seems even more to oppose the indifferent character of the society as symbolized by the Sunday congregation. The boat-house is one of the most important elements of the whole book, even for the impression it makes upon David, who is filled with the romantic idea of living in it. *"That ship-looking thing"* provided a perfect abode, precisely because it was originally meant as a boat. It represents the possibility of protection everywhere, which is the same when children build temporary nests under tables, another object meant for a different use. Besides this, the boat is built for movement so that its reversal to a house makes it even more surprising as a gift. Faery tale happiness fills this chapter, with all of nature supporting it — *"to hear the wind getting up out at sea, to know that the fog was creeping over the desolate flat outside, and to look at the fire, and think that there was no house near but this one, and this one a boat, was like enchantment."*

Even inside this enchantment pain is foreshadowed by the Biblical paintings of the Sacrifice of Isaac, and Daniel in the den of lions. His suffering will be so great and unjust, that David's faith in life and goodness can be considered equal to martyrdom. Yet, in the boat-house of Pegotty's brother these Biblical subjects most of all reveal the identity of pious people, determined to endure peacefully and faithfully the hardship of their life.

In *"The Friendly Waiter And I"* (chapter 5, *"I Am Sent Away From Home"*) for the first time Davy appears inside a completely strange environment. Yet, Dickens could have chosen a different moment, if he wanted more emphasis to strangeness or suffering. The particular illustration continues the boy's story

16

as if floating above misfortune, choosing to bring in front of anything else his lovable character. In his eyes the hideous waiter appears playful. The same way we can 'read' the frames on the wall, not as underlining the boy's misfortune, rather belonging to a sort of headquarters, to help him start this hard exploration of the world from inside his never ending kindness. The illustration marks simultaneously the end of his first happy days and the days of agony.

In *"My Musical Breakfast"* Dickens and Phiz manage to depict the essence of the chapter as described by the title (*"I Am Sent Away from Home"*). 'Away from home' truly means being an unwanted stranger, and this is how Davy feels for the first time in these illustrations — neglected, between an old woman who cares for nothing but the fire, and the mother of his teacher adoring the son no matter how awfully he played the flute, as if only to emphasize the absence of his own mother. Even his hat is thrown and left alone on the floor...

An interesting detail, although impossible to appear in the illustration, is that all of Davy's misery came to surface only when his teacher played the flute. The boy was able until then to enjoy his meal. This cannot be interpreted as a sort of aestheticism, the awful music in perfect agreement with Davy's life, became simultaneously an extension, reminder and intensification of his pain. In *"Steerforth and Mr. Mell"* (chapter 7, *"My 'First Half' at Salem House"*), an etching with so many boys in all sorts of moods, David is the only person in the classroom that looks down to the ground. We are introduced to Steerforth's arrogance and cruelty, even more striking compared with Davy's exhaustion.

"Changes At Home" (chapter 8, *"My Holidays. Especially One Happy After-noon"*), as was said above depicts a moment of pure happiness; his mother is still alive and he even has the chance to feel 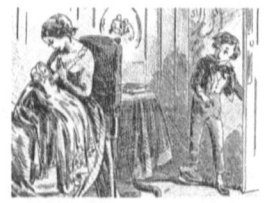 and witness in the affection for the newborn child her love for himself. Davy is again, more than ever, at home.

"Mrs. Gummidge Casts A Damp On Our Departure" (from chapter 10, *"I Become Neglected, And Am Provided For"*), an etching full of joyous movement, treasures one more happy moment of David's life, connected with the caring and festive Yarmouth family. We see at last the exterior of the boat-house in front of the sea, a tragic moment too, since Davy now has to follow the opposite direction, *"at the house, in which there was no face to look on mine with love or liking any more."*

"My Magnificent Order At The Public-House" (chapter 11, *"I Begin Life On My Own Account, And Don't Like It"*) isolates a moment that tries to be pleasurable, with David ordering a drink and discovering the owners ready to treat him with kindness. However, seeing him at that age in front of gigantic barrels to get beer for a special occasion he is going to 'celebrate' alone, cannot be a source of satisfaction. In the course of time life made him expect everything, yet he admits *"it is matter of some surprise to me, even now, that I can have been so easily thrown away at such an age"*. David needs nothing more than his home, and the next etching depicts his decision to find it.

In *"I Make Myself Known To My Aunt"* (from chapter 13, *"The Sequel Of My Resolution"*) Phiz had to present one of the most important moments in the whole novel, when the boy tries his last chance for a way back to intimacy, resorting to aunt Betsey after a long and painful trip, *"sustained and led on* by my fanciful picture of my mother in her youth, before I came into the world. It always kept me company. It was there, among the hops, when I lay down to sleep; it was with me on my waking in the morning; it went before me all day." In front of a house that exhibits female comfort, caring surprise answers his sorrow and exhaustion, among country kids and donkeys. Bright light enters his life again.

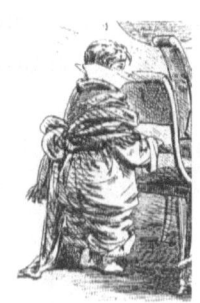 In *"The Momentous Interview"* (from chapter 14, *"My Aunt Makes Up Her Mind About Me"*) we are inside the house, where Mr. Dick warm, big and joyful stands like a strong guardian that the Murdstones could not ignore. David is tied and protected near his Aunt as if in a castle. In this illustration the viewer enjoys for the first time a complete relief that the boy found at last a house, in which there was a face to look on his with love or liking. He can't believe a real life is ahead for him, and he does not want even to remember the past, *"Now that the state of doubt was over, I felt, for many days, like one in a dream. ... The two things clearest in my mind were, that a remoteness had come upon the old Blunderstone life — which seemed to lie in the haze of an immeasurable distance; and that a curtain had for ever fallen on my life at Murdstone and Grinby's. No one has ever raised that curtain since. I have lifted it for a moment, even in this narrative, with a reluctant hand, and dropped it gladly. The remembrance of that life is fraught with so much pain to me, with so much mental suffering and want of hope, that I have never had the courage even to examine how long I was doomed to lead it..."*

"I Return To The Doctor's After The Party" (from chapter 16, *"I Am A New Boy In More Senses Than One"*) marks the end of the boy's trouble by sending him to the background while

other themes emerge — he is becoming an observer, and he discovers his first topic in the love between Doctor Strong and Annie, strange as he understands it, a love that somehow overcomes their difference in age.

Then *"Somebody Turns Up"* (chapter 17, by the same title), and is disappointed facing his friend's back. Uriah's mother like Mr. Mell's adores her son without any reason at all, rather despite the reasons that beg for the exact opposite. David is absorbed by Uriah in a way that makes him cold, rude, almost hostile, able to ignore a good old friend like Mr. Mikawber. Hard to accept even temporary corruption in a heart like his. This illustration and, in some ambiguity, the next one, narrate some disappointment with David himself.

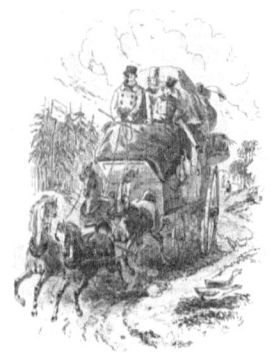

"My First Fall In Life" (from chapter 19, *"I Look About Me And Make A Discovery"*) is exquisite for the glorious movement of the horses and the overall arrangement of directions expanding like radiance. David's first fall is what he understands as cowardice, without excusing himself for his age or suspecting himself for arrogance. Phiz and Dickens accept his disposition as a wish to enjoy his improved social standing, especially because sad memories still haunt him.

"We Arrive Unexpectedly At Mr. Peggotty's Fireside" (from chapter 21, *"Little Em'ly"*) gives another chance to get inside the boat-house. David and Steerforth, still in the darkness of the open air, seem almost like intruders and are attracted by the clapping of Mrs. Gummidge to the main incident, little Emily in a field of love extending to her by Ham, Mr. Pegotty and Mrs. Gummidge. The etching presents a paradise little Emily

would have to lose and find anew. David becomes the catalyst for great changes in the life of others.

Miss Mowcher shows up at the center of *"I Make The Acquaintance Of Miss Mowcher"* (chapter 22, *"Some Old Scenes, And Some New People"*) like a creature of a new species. In her affection this impossible being almost personifies the ground of Steerforth's haughtiness.

In *"Martha"* (from the same chapter, 22) Phiz once more illustrates depression. David is almost a shadow, completely in the background, while Martha stays kneeled covering her face in her hand. No one is able to give her the slightest comfort.

Contrary to the previous illustration, this one, *"Uriah Persists In Hovering Near Us, At The Dinner-Party"* (from chapter 25, *"Good And Bad Angels"*) depicts a scene that is partly merry despite all formality. David leans toward Agnes while Uriah observes unnoticed like some bird of prey. Innocence and nobility under attack.

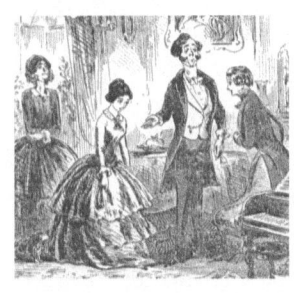

"I Fall Into Captivity" (from chapter 26, by the same title) features spontaneous affection against the artificial pride of servants, recognizing in love the most important property of freedom. David understands himself as a captive, but we witness the opposite, his freedom becoming stronger.

"We Are Disturbed In Our Cookery" (chapter 28, *"Mr. Micawber's Gauntlet"*) makes of David an example, in the contrast between his gentle, orderly, quiet and friendly life and Steerforth's shallowness being a source of problems to himself and to those who care about and look after him.

"I Find Mr. Barkis Going Out With The Tide" (from chap-

ter 30, *"A Loss"*), makes a comment on death. Clara, Dan'l and David are looking at Barkis, as is natural, with Clara staying close to his head speaking to him, and the two men a little further. Barkis is hugging his trunk, as if caressing all of his years in this life, sad to be separated from a whole life that he loved. The etching matches perfectly the *"going out with the tide"* metaphor as Barkis is being carried away from this life by a force that surpasses his will.

"Mr. Peggotty And Mrs. Steerforth" (chapter 32, *"The Beginning Of A Long Journey"*) meet each other in their affection and worry, and are also separated by their class and the criticism of each other's child. Contrary to Rosa, blindly following the Steerforths, David reflects this strange unity and separation, by seating-without-seating, in reality being the only one without a real position. The two parents are firmly defined by class and interest, David is mainly occupied with himself, being close to both Emily and Steerforth he is uneasy, undecided, unable to give himself to a complete feeling.

"My Aunt Astonishes Me" (from chapter 34, by the same title) pictures a detached way to face bad news. The prominent position of the kite signifies that David became and still remains the center of a world that is now bankrupt and in need of him. David is always above anything else a child in this world, his aunt keeping all authority, although not all responsibility for what should be done to overcome the sudden trouble.

"Mr. Wickfield And His Partner Wait Upon My Aunt" (from chapter 35, *"Depression"*) introduces the surrendered face of depression simultaneously with the cause of it in the hideous personality of Uriah Heep. Wickfield's noble character is emphasized even more in Agnes' and Betsey's care for him, while at the left David seems almost like a guardian as he keeps to

some distance Uriah bending in the quasi-joy of a demon.

After the gloomy intrusion of Uriah Heep in David's circle, *"Mr. Micawber Delivers Some Valedictory Remarks"* (from chapter 36, *"Enthousiasm"*) brings a great relief, with Micawber standing happy, David staring at him innocent, careful and direct like a child, Traddles being merry, Micawber's wife sensing her husband's attention.

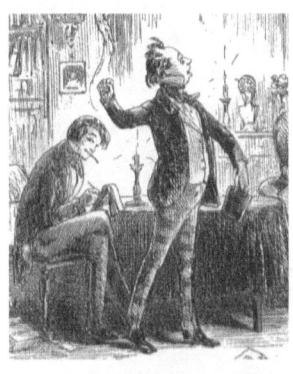

In *"Traddles Makes A Figure In Parliament, And I Report Him"* (chapter 38, *"A Dissolution Of Partnership"*) we are again happily in the very close circle of David, in his sitting-room, with David and Traddles exercising themselves for the start of their career. A sense of modernity is present in the posture of David accompanying youthful joy and hope.

"The Wanderer" (from chapter 40, by the same title) returns to the dark side of these illustrations, following Daniel Peggoty's search for Emily. Martha appears almost like a shadow or ghost at the back. Again David exists as if only to let others show up and play a part, like a catalyst.

"Traddles And I In Conference With The Misses Spenlow" (from chapter 41, *"Dora's Aunts"*) introduces to the forthcoming marriage of David with Dora, presenting his eager personality in contrast with the living wall of Dora's relatives, a formality he must overcome — or perhaps an allusion to the world that gave birth to his darling girl.

"I Am Married" (chapter 43, *"Another Retrospect"*) makes a reference to the first in this series of illustrations, *"Our Pew at Church"*. David's marriage with Dora seems to start a new cir-

cle in his life, in a moment of happiness and hope, with himself being the primary source of decisions that shape his future. The previous illustration regarded the interior of the church while this one the movement of the couple to enter their common life, as if the boy David after all those years now for the first time really leaves his childhood.

The next illustration, *"Our Housekeeping"* (chapter 44, by the same title) shows the couple in a home that never suffered this lack of order, even when David was a bachelor! I don't know if author and illustrator meant the etching to be 'fun,' it is sad, with a clouded David, and a Dora that suffers a guilty conscience. The couple's life seems far from an ideal inspiration for David's creative forces.

In *"Mr. Dick Fulfils My Aunt's Prediction"* (from chapter 45, by the same title) David remains in the dark of the room along with aunt Betsey, witnessing Mr. Dick's wise support of Dr. Strong's relationship with Annie. There is something superficial and embarrassing in this illustration and the relevant part of the novel — such an important personal moment among so many visitors!

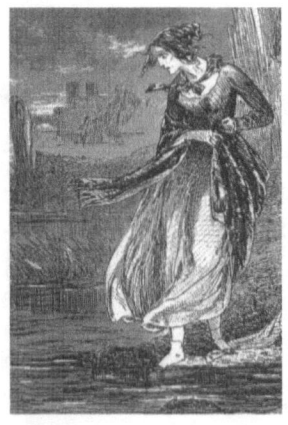

Although her figure is prominent, *"The River"* (chapter 47, *"Martha"*) is wisely named after the destination of Martha's despair, thus avoiding her complete identification with this development, suggesting her to be something more. The figures at the back represent life, care and hope, even a bright side of her own past, thus being totally irrelevant in that moment of darkness and isolation. They stop her now, but will she be saved, find a destination more meaningful than the mud of the river?

"Mr. Peggotty's Dream Comes True" (from chapter 50, by the same title) pictures a sorry and frightened David, as in the previous illustration, although this time all danger has become a girl in need of immediate solace and a recollection of the past. In the hands of Mr. Peggotty Emily starts returning to the white years of her childhood.

In *"Restoration Of Mutual Confidence Between Mr. And Mrs. Micawber"* (chapter 52, *"I Assist At An Explosion"*), David and his closest persons, Betsey and Mr. Dick, remaining in the background share the joy of the Micawbers. The older boy, at the left, stays calm beside his flute, an exception of thoughtfulness and sobriety in his family.

In *"My Child-Wife's Old Companion"* (from chapter 53, *"Another Retrospect"*), Dora starts to become a memory, appearing only in the frame on the wall, her guitar leaning against her empty chair just for a while before it is removed, her dog dying... and inside David's sorrow his new wife already comes into view. Although the picture is about loss, the presence of Agnes in a memory so full of Dora, makes it really crowded.

In *"I Am The Bearer Of Evil Tidings"* (from chapter 56, *"The New Wound, And The Old"*), the bearer is more affected by the evil tidings than Steerforth's own mother, a contrast between those who have warm feelings or the freedom to express them, and those who think they are obliged to protect their 'highness.'

In *"The Emigrants"* (chapter 57, by the same title) Mr. Mikawber appears for the last time in these illustrations, the only person, among a lot of emigrants, being excited like an explorer. Almost everyone in the picture looks down making the ambitious departure of Micawber's family even more impressive.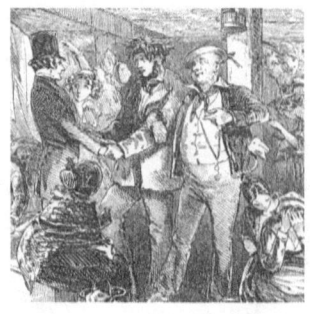

"I Am Shown Two Interesting Penitents" (from chapter 61, by the same title) features fraudulence, not in the sense of scheming, but of a hideous attraction to falsity whether the others understand it as such or not, i.e. absolute lack of interest in anything genuine and true.

"A Stranger Calls To See Me" (from chapter 63, *"A Visitor"*) ends the series of the David Copperfield illustrations with David and especially Mr. Pegotty much older. David and Agnes enjoy their family life in front of the fire among children, books and dolls, when Mr. Pegotty lets David's past enter the room, caressing his offspring and fulfilling the blessing. Even Dora's memory is still alive, and the boat-house, where David first met with the Pegottys and knew a special kind of magic.

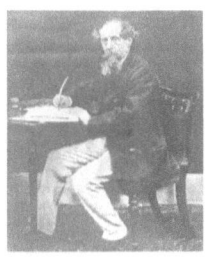 Textual description tends to abstraction, the reader has to imagine a lot, a sense of uncertainty develops in the necessary arbitrariness, and a substantial level of abstraction still remains. A picture presents exact distances, shapes, relations, expressions, sizes... leaving less to be decided by the reader.

Letting a few images inside his texts, Dickens added a level of concrete and certain reality, a visual aid that would help his readers imagine better and stay closer to the world of the book.

A replacement of the text with images, as in the "Classical Illustrated" series, is rightly considered 'easy reading,' closer to the art of movies, when visual representation or a reality easily shared, comes above the level of thinking, imagination and freedom; this would betray the powers of Dickens' writing, as is obvious in the numerous Dickens movies today, able to transmit not much more than the atmosphere of Victorian London and a basic sense of the plot and characters.

Yet the use of illustrations in a novel of the highest quality helps to understand a balance that is able to stimulate our mind. Without any images our perception is filled first by the neutral uniform appearance of letters, words, paragraphs, to achieve the above described mixture of abstraction and imagination. This aspect of reading favors the understanding of ideas and the dominance of the plot. Intelligence is strengthened.

Allowing a small number of illustrations Dickens did not damage the virtues of reading, he kept all the benefits of a poetical reality that is expressed in pure text, enhancing abstract reasoning and imagination with drops of immediacy, little windows by which the certainty of our everyday vision finds a way to unite with the text, making fiction appear even closer to reality, supporting the sense of completeness.

The discreet visual element of these images is incorporated in the novel representing our sensual perception, without hindering the freedom of participating in the wealth of ideas, interpretations, suggestions and all the subtleties inherent in a text.

THE PHIZ ILLUSTRATIONS OF
DAVID COPPERFIELD

With Chapter Excerpts

Our Pew At Church

From Chapter II: "I Observe"

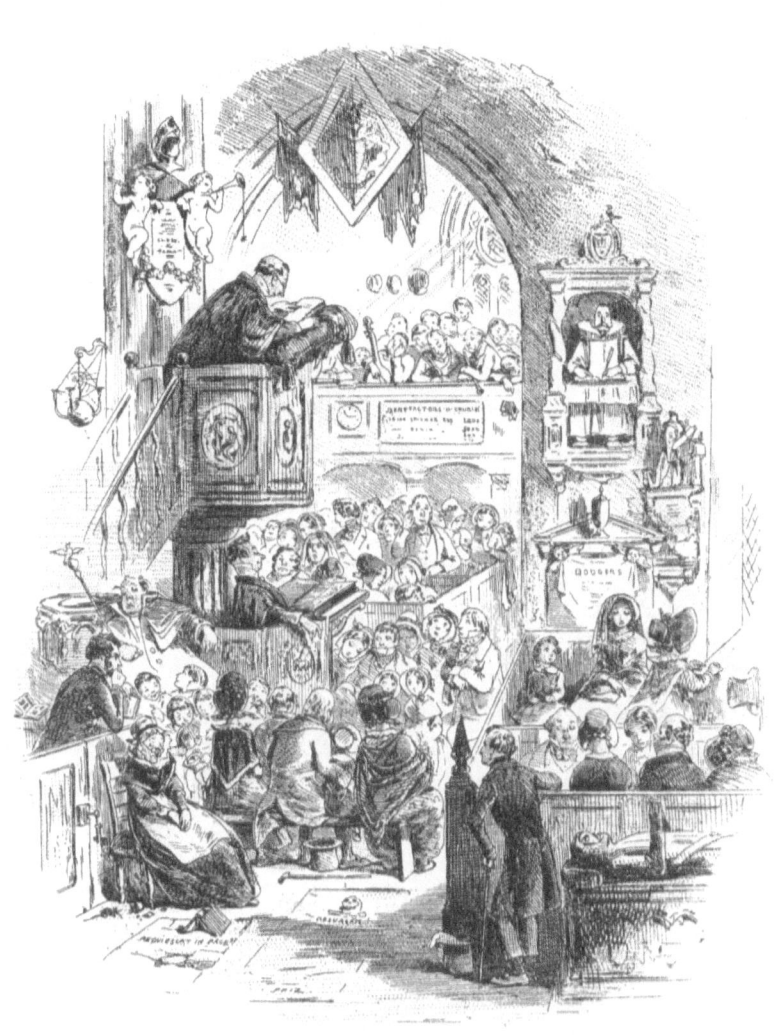

There is nothing half so green that I know any-where, as the grass of that churchyard; nothing half so shady as its trees; nothing half so quiet as its tombstones. The sheep are feeding there, when I kneel up, early in the morning, in my little bed in a closet within my mother's room, to look out at it; and I see the red light shining on the sun-dial, and think within myself, 'Is the sun-dial glad, I wonder, that it can tell the time again?'

Here is our pew in the church. What a high-backed pew! With a window near it, out of which our house can be seen, and IS seen many times during the morning's service, by Peggotty, who likes to make herself as sure as she can that it's not being robbed, or is not in flames. But though Peggotty's eye wanders, she is much offended if mine does, and frowns to me, as I stand upon the seat, that I am to look at the clergyman. But I can't always look at him – I know him without that white thing on, and I am afraid of his wondering why I stare so, and perhaps stopping the service to inquire – and what am I to do? It's a dreadful thing to gape, but I must do something. I look at my mother, but she pretends not to see me. I look at a boy in the aisle, and he makes faces at me. I look at the sunlight coming in at the open door through the porch, and there I see a stray sheep – I don't mean a sinner, but mutton – half making up his mind to come into the church. I feel that if I looked at him any longer, I might be tempted to say something out loud; and what would become of me then! I look up at the monumental tablets on the wall, and try to think of Mr. Bodgers late of this parish, and what the feelings of Mrs. Bodgers must have been, when affliction sore, long time Mr. Bodgers bore, and physicians were in vain. I wonder whether they called in Mr. Chillip, and he was in vain; and if so, how he likes to be reminded of it once a week. I look from Mr. Chillip, in his Sunday neckcloth, to the pulpit;

and think what a good place it would be to play in, and what a castle it would make, with another boy coming up the stairs to attack it, and having the velvet cushion with the tassels thrown down on his head. In time my eyes gradually shut up; and, from seeming to hear the clergyman singing a drowsy song in the heat, I hear nothing, until I fall off the seat with a crash, and am taken out, more dead than alive, by Peggotty.

And now I see the outside of our house, with the latticed bedroom-windows standing open to let in the sweet-smelling air, and the ragged old rooks'-nests still dangling in the elm-trees at the bottom of the front garden. Now I am in the garden at the back, beyond the yard where the empty pigeon-house and dog-kennel are – a very preserve of butterflies, as I remember it, with a high fence, and a gate and padlock; where the fruit clusters on the trees, riper and richer than fruit has ever been since, in any other garden, and where my mother gathers some in a basket, while I stand by, bolting furtive gooseberries, and trying to look unmoved. A great wind rises, and the summer is gone in a moment. We are playing in the winter twilight, dancing about the parlour. When my mother is out of breath and rests herself in an elbow-chair, I watch her winding her bright curls round her fingers, and straitening her waist, and nobody knows better than I do that she likes to look so well, and is proud of being so pretty.

I Am Hospitably Received By Mr. Peggotty

From Chapter III: "I Have A Change"

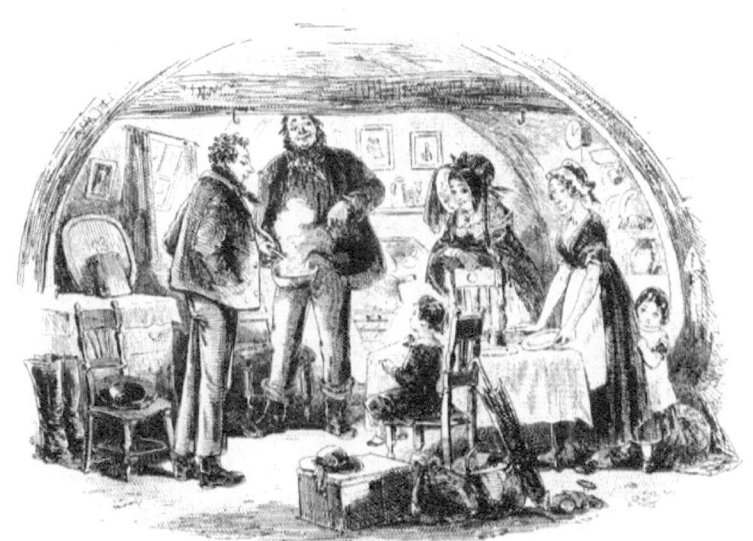

on's our house, Mas'r Davy!'

I looked in all directions, as far as I could stare over the wilderness, and away at the sea, and away at the river, but no house could I make out. There was a black barge, or some other kind of superannuated boat, not far off, high and dry on the ground, with an iron funnel sticking out of it for a chimney and smoking very cosily; but nothing else in the way of a habitation that was visible to me.

'That's not it?' said I. 'That ship-looking thing?'

'That's it, Mas'r Davy,' returned Ham.

If it had been Aladdin's palace, roc's egg and all, I suppose I could not have been more charmed with the romantic idea of living in it. There was a delightful door cut in the side, and it was roofed in, and there were little windows in it; but the wonderful charm of it was, that it was a real boat which had no doubt been upon the water hundreds of times, and which had never been intended to be lived in, on dry land. That was the captivation of it to me. If it had ever been meant to be lived in, I might have thought it small, or inconvenient, or lonely; but never having been designed for any such use, it became a perfect abode.

It was beautifully clean inside, and as tidy as possible. There was a table, and a Dutch clock, and a chest of drawers, and on the chest of drawers there was a tea-tray with a painting on it of a lady with a parasol, taking a walk with a military-looking child who was trundling a hoop. The tray was kept from tumbling down, by a bible; and the tray, if it had tumbled down, would have smashed a quantity of cups and saucers and a teapot that were grouped around the book. On the walls there were some common coloured pictures, framed and glazed, of scripture subjects; such as I have never seen since in the hands of pedlars, without seeing the whole interior of Peggotty's brother's house again, at one view. Abraham in red going to sacrifice Isaac in blue, and Daniel in yellow cast into a den of green lions, were the most prominent of these. Over the little mantelshelf, was a picture of the 'Sarah Jane' lugger, built at Sunderland, with a real little wooden stern stuck on to it; a work of art, combining composition with carpentry, which I considered to be one of the most enviable possessions that the world could afford. There were some hooks in the beams of the ceiling, the use of which I did not divine then; and some lockers and boxes and conveniences of that sort, which served for seats and eked out the chairs.

All this I saw in the first glance after I crossed the threshold – child-like, according to my theory – and then Peggotty opened a little door and showed me my bedroom. It was the completest and most desirable bedroom ever seen – in the stern of the vessel; with a little window, where the rudder used to go through; a little looking-glass, just the right height for me, nailed against the wall, and framed with oyster-shells; a little bed, which there was just room enough to get into; and a nosegay of seaweed in a blue mug on the table. The walls were whitewashed as white as milk, and the patchwork counterpane made my eyes quite ache with its brightness. One thing I particularly noticed in this delightful house, was the smell of fish; which was so searching, that when I took out my pocket-handkerchief to wipe my nose, I found it smelt exactly as if it had wrapped up a lobster. On my imparting this discovery in confidence to Peggotty, she informed me that her brother dealt in lobsters, crabs, and crawfish; and I afterwards found that a heap of these creatures, in a state of wonderful conglomeration with one another, and never leaving off pinching whatever they laid hold of, were usually to be found in a little wooden outhouse where the pots and kettles were kept.

We were welcomed by a very civil woman in a white apron,

whom I had seen curtseying at the door when I was on Ham's back, about a quarter of a mile off. Likewise by a most beautiful little girl (or I thought her so) with a necklace of blue beads on, who wouldn't let me kiss her when I offered to, but ran away and hid herself. By and by, when we had dined in a sumptuous manner off boiled dabs, melted butter, and potatoes, with a chop for me, a hairy man with a very good-natured face came home. As he called Peggotty 'Lass', and gave her a hearty smack on the cheek, I had no doubt, from the general propriety of her conduct, that he was her brother; and so he turned out – being presently introduced to me as Mr. Peggotty, the master of the house.

'Glad to see you, sir,' said Mr. Peggotty. 'You'll find us rough, sir, but you'll find us ready.'

I thanked him, and replied that I was sure I should be happy in such a delightful place.

'How's your Ma, sir?' said Mr. Peggotty. 'Did you leave her pretty jolly?'

I gave Mr. Peggotty to understand that she was as jolly as I could wish, and that she desired her compliments – which was a polite fiction on my part.

'I'm much obleeged to her, I'm sure,' said Mr. Peggotty. 'Well, sir, if you can make out here, fur a fortnut, 'long wi' her,' nodding at his sister, 'and Ham, and little Em'ly, we shall be proud of your company.'

Having done the honours of his house in this hospitable manner, Mr. Peggotty went out to wash himself in a kettleful of hot water, remarking that 'cold would never get his muck off'. He soon returned, greatly improved in appearance; but so rubicund, that I couldn't help thinking his face had this in common with the lobsters, crabs, and crawfish, – that it went into the hot *water very black, and came out very red.*

After tea, when the door was shut and all was made snug (the nights being cold and misty now), it seemed to me the most delicious retreat that the imagination of man could conceive. To hear the wind getting up out at sea, to know that the fog was creeping over the desolate flat outside, and to look at the fire, and think that there was no house near but this one, and this one a boat, was like enchantment.

The Friendly Waiter And I

From Chapter V: "I Am Sent Away From Home"

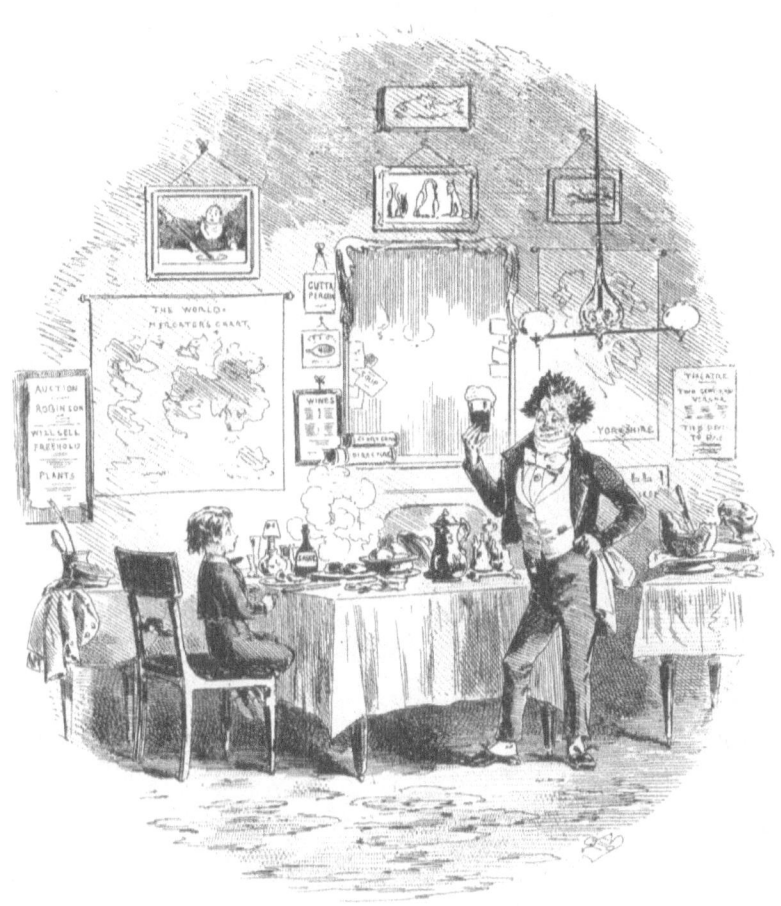

*I*t was a large long room with some large maps in it. I doubt if I could have felt much stranger if the maps had been real foreign countries, and I cast away in the middle of them. I felt it was taking a liberty to sit down, with my cap in my hand, on the corner of the chair nearest the door; and when the waiter laid a cloth on purpose for me, and put a set of castors on it, I think I must have turned red all over with modesty.

He brought me some chops, and vegetables, and took the covers off in such a bouncing manner that I was afraid I must have given him some offence. But he greatly relieved my mind by putting a chair for me at the table, and saying, very affably, 'Now, six-foot! come on!'

I thanked him, and took my seat at the board; but found it extremely difficult to handle my knife and fork with anything like dexterity, or to avoid splashing myself with the gravy, while he was standing opposite, staring so hard, and making me blush in the most dreadful manner every time I caught his eye. After watching me into the second chop, he said:

'There's half a pint of ale for you. Will you have it now?'

I thanked him and said, 'Yes.' Upon which he poured it out of a jug into a large tumbler, and held it up against the light, and made it look beautiful.

'My eye!' he said. 'It seems a good deal, don't it?'

'It does seem a good deal,' I answered with a smile. For it was quite delightful to me, to find him so pleasant. He was a twinkling-eyed, pimple-faced man, with his hair standing upright all over his head; and as he stood with one arm a-kimbo, holding up the glass to the light with the other hand, he looked quite friendly.

My Musical Breakfast

From Chapter V: "I Am Sent Away From Home"

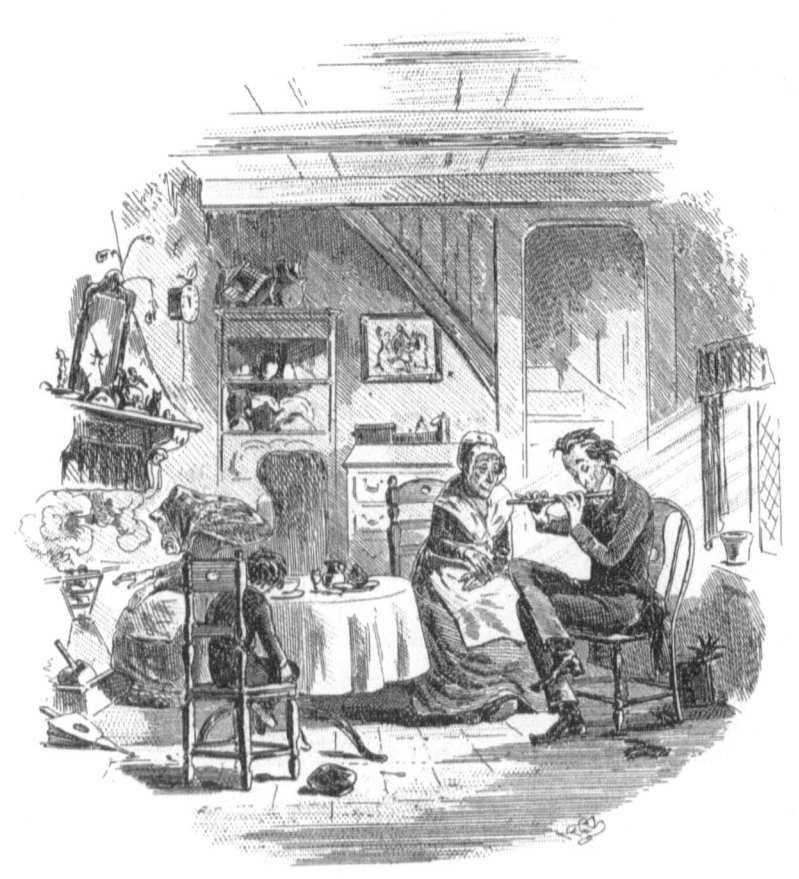

*A*lthough it was a warm day, she seemed to think of nothing but the fire. I fancied she was jealous even of the saucepan on it; and I have reason to know that she took its impressment into the service of boiling my egg and broiling my bacon, in dudgeon; for I saw her, with my own discomfited eyes, shake her fist at me once, when those culinary operations were going on, and no one else was looking. The sun streamed in at the little window, but she sat with her own back and the back of the large chair towards it, screening the fire as if she were sedulously keeping IT warm, instead of it keeping her warm, and watching it in a most distrustful manner. The completion of the preparations for my breakfast, by relieving the fire, gave her such extreme joy that she laughed aloud – and a very unmelodious laugh she had, I must say.

I sat down to my brown loaf, my egg, and my rasher of bacon, with a basin of milk besides, and made a most delicious meal. While I was yet in the full enjoyment of it, the old woman of the house said to the Master:

'Have you got your flute with you?'

'Yes,' he returned.

'Have a blow at it,' said the old woman, coaxingly. 'Do!'

The Master, upon this, put his hand underneath the skirts of his coat, and brought out his flute in three pieces, which he screwed together, and began immediately to play. My impression is, after many years of consideration, that there never can have been anybody in the world who played worse. He made the most dismal sounds I have ever heard produced by any means, natural or artificial. I don't know what the tunes were – if there were such things in the performance at all, which I doubt – but the influence of the strain upon me was, first, to make me think of all my sorrows until I could hardly keep my tears back; then to take away my appetite; and lastly, to make me so sleepy that I couldn't keep my eyes open. They begin to close again, and I begin to nod, as the recollection rises fresh upon me. Once more the little room, with its open corner cupboard, and its square-backed chairs, and its angular little staircase leading to the room above, and its three peacock's feathers displayed over the mantel-piece — I remember wondering when I first went in, what that peacock would have thought if he had known what his finery was doomed to come to — fades from before me, and I nod, and sleep. The flute becomes inaudible, the wheels of the coach are heard instead, and I am on my journey. The coach jolts, I wake with a start, and the flute has come back again, and the Master at Salem House is sitting with his legs crossed, playing it doleful-ly, while the old woman of the house looks on delighted. She fades in her turn, and he fades, and all fades, and there is no flute, no Master, no Salem House, no David Copperfield, no anything but heavy sleep.

I dreamed, I thought, that once while he was blowing into this dismal flute, the old woman of the house, who had gone nearer and nearer to him in her ecstatic admiration, leaned over the back of his chair and gave him an affectionate squeeze round the neck, which stopped his playing for a moment. I was in the middle state between sleeping and waking, either then or immediately afterwards; for, as he resumed — it was a real fact that he had stopped playing — I saw and heard the same old woman ask Mrs. Fibbitson if it wasn't delicious (meaning the flute), to which Mrs. Fibbitson replied, 'Ay, ay! yes!' and nodded at the fire: to which, I am persuaded, she gave the credit of the whole performance.

Steerforth And Mr. Mell

From Chapter VII: "My 'First Half' At Salem House"

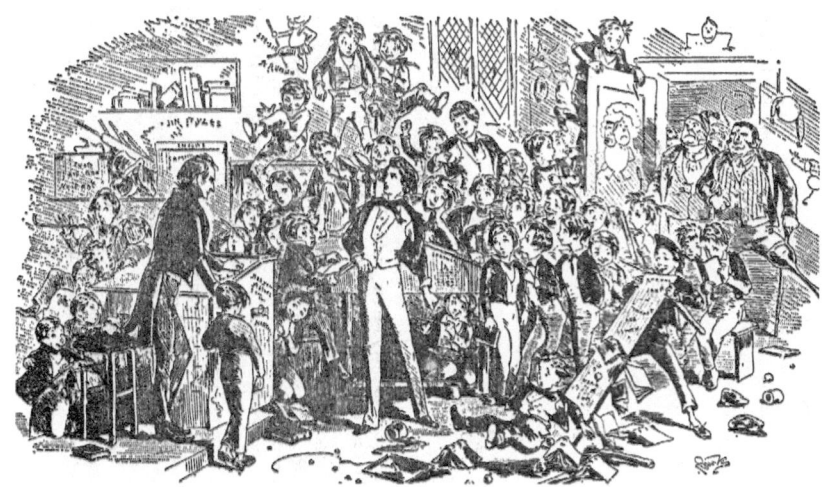

*I*t was, properly, a half-holiday; being Saturday. But as the noise in the playground would have disturbed Mr. Creakle, and the weather was not favourable for going out walking, we were ordered into school in the afternoon, and set some lighter tasks than usual, which were made for the occasion. It was the day of the week on which Mr. Sharp went out to get his wig curled; so Mr. Mell, who always did the drudgery, whatever it was, kept school by himself. If I could associate the idea of a bull or a bear with anyone so mild as Mr. Mell, I should think of him, in connexion with that afternoon when the uproar was at its height, as of one of those animals, baited by a thousand dogs. I recall him bending his aching head, supported on his bony hand, over the book on his desk, and wretchedly endeavouring to get on with his tiresome work, amidst an uproar that might have made the Speaker of the House of Commons giddy. Boys started in and out of their places, playing at puss in the corner with other boys; there were laughing boys, singing boys, talking boys, dancing boys, howling boys; boys shuffled with their feet, boys whirled about him, grinning, making faces, mimicking him behind his back and before his eyes; mimicking his poverty, his boots, his coat, his mother, everything belonging to him that they should have had consideration for.

'Silence!' cried Mr. Mell, suddenly rising up, and striking his desk with the book. 'What does this mean! It's impossible to bear it. It's maddening. How can you do it to me, boys?'

It was my book that he struck his desk with; and as I stood beside him, following his eye as it glanced round the room, I saw the boys all stop, some suddenly surprised, some half afraid, and some sorry perhaps.

Steerforth's place was at the bottom of the school, at the opposite end of the long room. He was lounging with his back against the wall, and his hands in his pockets, and looked at Mr. Mell with his mouth shut up as if he were whistling, when Mr. Mell looked at him.

'Silence, Mr. Steerforth!' said Mr. Mell.

'Silence yourself,' said Steerforth, turning red. 'Whom are you talking to?'

'Sit down,' said Mr. Mell.

'Sit down yourself,' said Steerforth, 'and mind your business.'

There was a titter, and some applause; but Mr. Mell was so white, that silence immediately succeeded; and one boy, who had darted out behind him to imitate his mother again, changed his mind, and pretended to want a pen mended.

'If you think, Steerforth,' said Mr. Mell, 'that I am not acquainted with the power you can establish over any mind here' – he laid his hand, without considering what he did (as I supposed), upon my head – 'or that I have not observed you, within a few minutes, urging your juniors on to every sort of outrage against me, you are mistaken.'

'I don't give myself the trouble of thinking at all about you,' said Steerforth, coolly; 'so I'm not mistaken, as it happens.'

'And when you make use of your position of favouritism here, sir,' pursued Mr. Mell, with his lip trembling very much, 'to insult a gentleman -'

'A what? – where is he?' said Steerforth.

Here somebody cried out, 'Shame, J. Steerforth! Too bad!' It was Traddles; whom Mr. Mell instantly discomfited by bidding him hold his tongue.

- 'To insult one who is not fortunate in life, sir, and who

never gave you the least offence, and the many reasons for not insulting whom you are old enough and wise enough to understand,' said Mr. Mell, with his lips trembling more and more, 'you commit a mean and base action. You can sit down or stand up as you please, sir. Copperfield, go on.'

'Young Copperfield,' said Steerforth, coming forward up the room, 'stop a bit. I tell you what, Mr. Mell, once for all. When you take the liberty of calling me mean or base, or anything of that sort, you are an impudent beggar. You are always a beggar, you know; but when you do that, you are an impudent beggar.'

I am not clear whether he was going to strike Mr. Mell, or Mr. Mell was going to strike him, or there was any such intention on either side. I saw a rigidity come upon the whole school as if they had been turned into stone, and found Mr. Creakle in the midst of us, with Tungay at his side, and Mrs. and Miss Creakle looking in at the door as if they were frightened. Mr. Mell, with his elbows on his desk and his face in his hands, sat, for some moments, quite still.

'Mr. Mell,' said Mr. Creakle, shaking him by the arm; and his whisper was so audible now, that Tungay felt it unnecessary to repeat his words; 'you have not forgotten yourself, I hope?'

'No, sir, no,' returned the Master, showing his face, and shaking his head, and rubbing his hands in great agitation. 'No, sir. No. I have remembered myself, I – no, Mr. Creakle, I have not forgotten myself, I – I have remembered myself, sir. I – I – could wish you had remembered me a little sooner, Mr. Creakle. It – it – would have been more kind, sir, more just, sir. It would have saved me something, sir.'

Mr. Creakle, looking hard at Mr. Mell, put his hand on Tungay's shoulder, and got his feet upon the form close by, and sat upon the desk. After still looking hard at Mr. Mell from his throne, as he shook his head, and rubbed his hands, and remained in the same state of agitation, Mr. Creakle turned to Steerforth, and said:

'Now, sir, as he don't condescend to tell me, what is this?'

Steerforth evaded the question for a little while; looking in scorn and anger on his opponent, and remaining silent. I could not help thinking even in that interval, I remember, what a noble fellow he was in appearance, and how homely and plain Mr. Mell looked opposed to him.

'What did he mean by talking about favourites, then?' said Steerforth at length.

'Favourites?' repeated Mr. Creakle, with the veins in his forehead swelling quickly. 'Who talked about favourites?'

'He did,' said Steerforth.

'And pray, what did you mean by that, sir?' demanded Mr. Creakle, turning angrily on his assistant.

'I meant, Mr. Creakle,' he returned in a low voice, 'as I said; that no pupil had a right to avail himself of his position of favouritism to degrade me.'

'To degrade YOU?' said Mr. Creakle. 'My stars! But give me leave to ask you, Mr. What's-your-name'; and here Mr. Creakle folded his arms, cane and all, upon his chest, and made such a knot of his brows that his little eyes were hardly visible below them; 'whether, when you talk about favourites, you showed proper respect to me? To me, sir,' said Mr. Creakle, darting his head at him suddenly, and drawing it back again, 'the principal of this establishment, and your employer.'

'It was not judicious, sir, I am willing to admit,' said Mr. Mell. 'I should not have done so, if I had been cool.'

Here Steerforth struck in.

'Then he said I was mean, and then he said I was base, and then I called him a beggar. If I had been cool, perhaps I shouldn't have called him a beggar. But I did, and I am ready to take the consequences of it.'

Without considering, perhaps, whether there were any consequences to be taken, I felt quite in a glow at this gallant speech. It made an impression on the boys too, for there was a low stir among them, though no one spoke a word.

'I am surprised, Steerforth – although your candour does you honour,' said Mr. Creakle, 'does you honour, certainly – I am surprised, Steerforth, I must say, that you should attach such an epithet to any person employed and paid in Salem House, sir.'

Steerforth gave a short laugh.

'That's not an answer, sir,' said Mr. Creakle, 'to my remark. I expect more than that from you, Steerforth.'

If Mr. Mell looked homely, in my eyes, before the handsome boy, it would be quite impossible to say how homely Mr. Creakle looked. 'Let him deny it,' said Steerforth.

'Deny that he is a beggar, Steerforth?' cried Mr. Creakle. 'Why, where does he go a-begging?'

'If he is not a beggar himself, his near relation's one,' said Steerforth. 'It's all the same.'

He glanced at me, and Mr. Mell's hand gently patted me upon the shoulder. I looked up with a flush upon my face and remorse in my heart, but Mr. Mell's eyes were fixed on Steerforth. He continued to pat me kindly on the shoulder, but he looked at him.

'Since you expect me, Mr. Creakle, to justify myself,' said Steerforth, 'and to say what I mean, – what I have to say is, that his mother lives on charity in an alms-house.'

Mr. Mell still looked at him, and still patted me kindly on the shoulder, and said to himself, in a whisper, if I heard right: 'Yes, I thought so.'

Mr. Creakle turned to his assistant, with a severe frown and laboured politeness:

'Now, you hear what this gentleman says, Mr. Mell. Have the goodness, if you please, to set him right before the assembled school.'

'He is right, sir, without correction,' returned Mr. Mell, in the midst of a dead silence; 'what he has said is true.'

'Be so good then as declare publicly, will you,' said Mr. Creakle, putting his head on one side, and rolling his eyes round the school, 'whether it ever came to my knowledge until this moment?'

'I believe not directly,' he returned.

'Why, you know not,' said Mr. Creakle. 'Don't you, man?'

'I apprehend you never supposed my worldly circumstances to be very good,' replied the assistant. 'You know what my position is, and always has been, here.'

'I apprehend, if you come to that,' said Mr. Creakle, with his veins swelling again bigger than ever, 'that you've been in a wrong position altogether, and mistook this for a charity school. Mr. Mell, we'll part, if you please. The sooner the better.'

'There is no time,' answered Mr. Mell, rising, 'like the present.'

'Sir, to you!' said Mr. Creakle.

'I take my leave of you, Mr. Creakle, and all of you,' said Mr. Mell, glancing round the room, and again patting me gently on the shoulders. 'James Steerforth, the best wish I can leave you is that you may come to be ashamed of what you have done

today. At present I would prefer to see you anything rather than a friend, to me, or to anyone in whom I feel an interest.'

Once more he laid his hand upon my shoulder; and then taking his flute and a few books from his desk, and leaving the key in it for his successor, he went out of the school, with his property under his arm. Mr. Creakle then made a speech, through Tungay, in which he thanked Steerforth for asserting (though perhaps too warmly) the independence and respectability of Salem House; and which he wound up by shaking hands with Steerforth, while we gave three cheers — I did not quite know what for, but I supposed for Steerforth, and so joined in them ardently, though I felt miserable. Mr. Creakle then caned Tommy Traddles for being discovered in tears, instead of cheers, on account of Mr. Mell's departure; and went back to his sofa, or his bed, or wherever he had come from.

Changes At Home

From Chapter VIII: "My Holidays. Especially One Happy Afternoon"

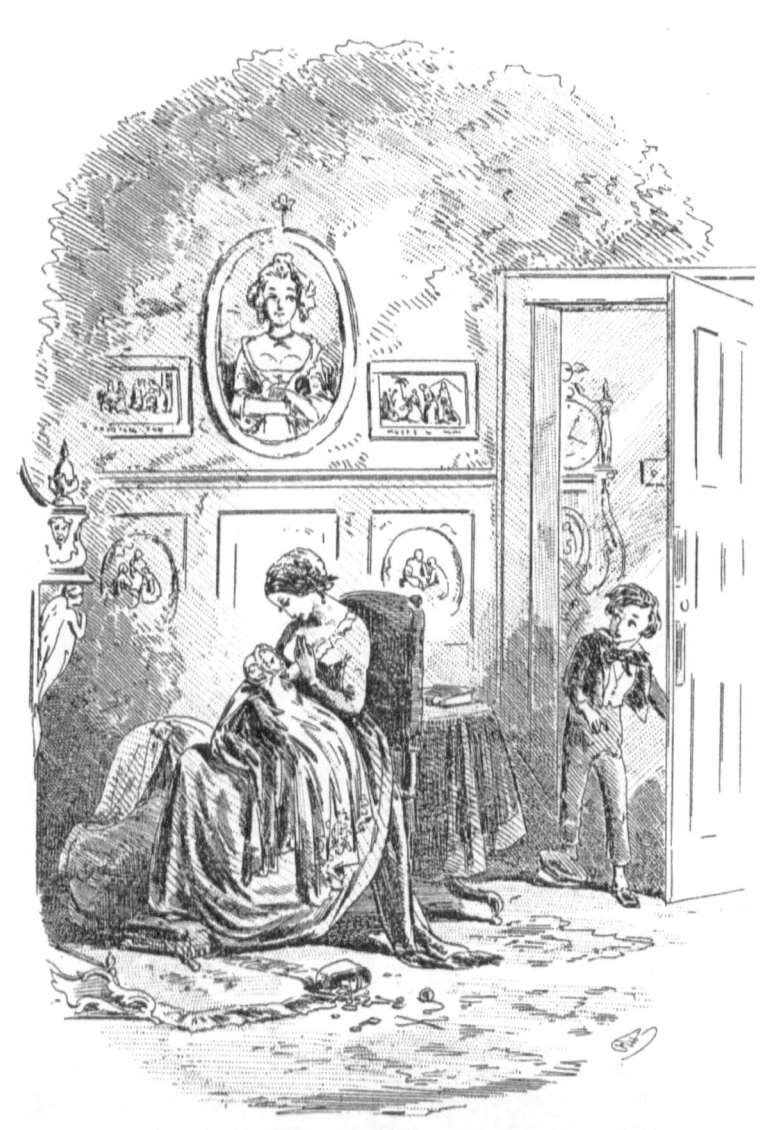

7 *he carrier put my box down at the garden-gate, and left me. I walked along the path towards the house, glancing at the windows, and fearing at every step to see Mr. Murdstone or Miss Murdstone lowering out of one of them. No face appeared, however; and being come to the house, and knowing how to open the door, before dark, without knocking, I went in with a quiet, timid step.*

God knows how infantine the memory may have been, that was awakened within me by the sound of my mother's voice in the old parlour, when I set foot in the hall. She was singing in a low tone. I think I must have lain in her arms, and heard her singing so to me when I was but a baby. The strain was new to me, and yet it was so old that it filled my heart brim-full; like a friend come back from a long absence.

I believed, from the solitary and thoughtful way in which my mother murmured her song, that she was alone. And I went softly into the room. She was sitting by the fire, suckling an infant, whose tiny hand she held against her neck. Her eyes were looking down upon its face, and she sat singing to it. I was so far right, that she had no other companion.

I spoke to her, and she started, and cried out. But seeing me, she called me her dear Davy, her own boy! and coming half across the room to meet me, kneeled down upon the ground and kissed me, and laid my head down on her bosom near the little creature that was nestling there, and put its hand to my lips.

I wish I had died. I wish I had died then, with that feeling in my heart! I should have been more fit for Heaven than I ever have been since.

Mrs. Gummidge Casts A Damp On Our Departure

From Chapter X: "I Become Neglected, And Am Provided For"

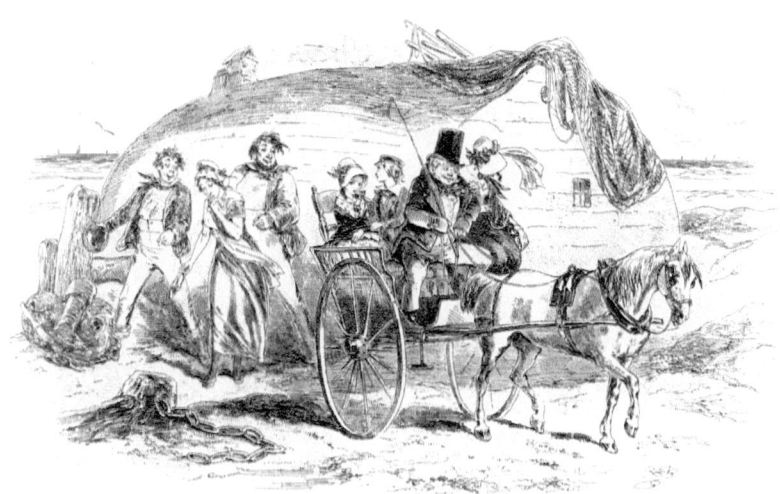

*A*t length, when the term of my visit was nearly expired, it was given out that Peggotty and Mr. Barkis were going to make a day's holiday together, and that little Em'ly and I were to accompany them. I had but a broken sleep the night before, in anticipation of the pleasure of a whole day with Em'ly. We were all astir betimes in the morning; and while we were yet at breakfast, Mr. Barkis appeared in the distance, driving a chaise-cart towards the object of his affections.

Peggotty was dressed as usual, in her neat and quiet mourning; but Mr. Barkis bloomed in a new blue coat, of which the tailor had given him such good measure, that the cuffs would have rendered gloves unnecessary in the coldest weather, while the collar was so high that it pushed his hair up on end on the top of his head. His bright buttons, too, were of the largest size. Rendered complete by drab pantaloons and a buff waistcoat, I thought Mr. Barkis a phenomenon of respectability.

When we were all in a bustle outside the door, I found that Mr. Peggotty was prepared with an old shoe, which was to be thrown after us for luck, and which he offered to Mrs. Gummidge for that purpose.

'No. It had better be done by somebody else, Dan'l,' said Mrs. Gummidge. 'I'm a lone lorn creetur' myself, and everythink that reminds me of creetur's that ain't lone and lorn, goes contrary with me.'

'Come, old gal!' cried Mr. Peggotty. 'Take and heave it.'

'No, Dan'l,' returned Mrs. Gummidge, whimpering and shaking her head. 'If I felt less, I could do more. You don't feel like me, Dan'l; thinks don't go contrary with you, nor you with them; you had better do it yourself.'

But here Peggotty, who had been going about from one to

another in a hurried way, kissing everybody, called out from the cart, in which we all were by this time (Em'ly and I on two little chairs, side by side), that Mrs. Gummidge must do it. So Mrs. Gummidge did it; and, I am sorry to relate, cast a damp upon the festive character of our departure, by immediately bursting into tears, and sinking subdued into the arms of Ham, with the declaration that she knowed she was a burden, and had better be carried to the House at once. Which I really thought was a sensible idea, that Ham might have acted on.

My Magnificent Order At The Public-House

From Chapter XI: "I Begin Life On My Own Account, And Don't Like It"

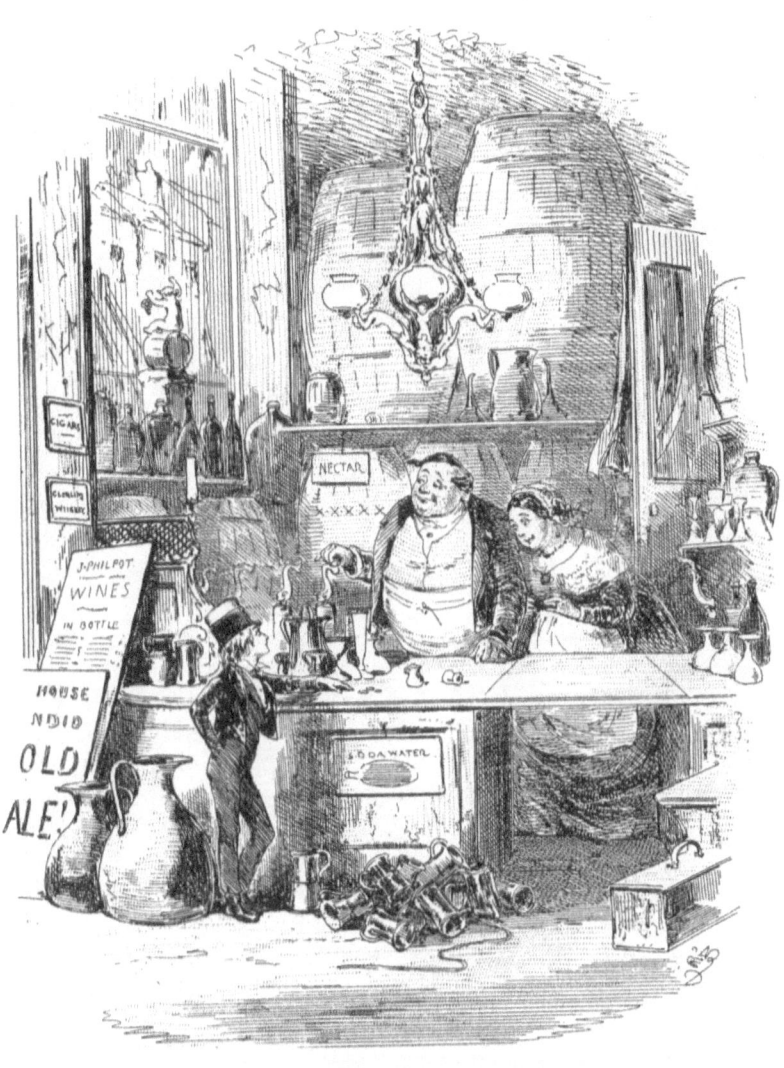

I was such a child, and so little, that frequently when I went into the bar of a strange public-house for a glass of ale or porter, to moisten what I had had for dinner, they were afraid to give it me. I remember one hot evening I went into the bar of a public-house, and said to the landlord: 'What is your best – your very best – ale a glass?' For it was a special occasion. I don't know what. It may have been my birthday.

'Twopence-halfpenny,' says the landlord, 'is the price of the Genuine Stunning ale.'

'Then,' says I, producing the money, 'just draw me a glass of the Genuine Stunning, if you please, with a good head to it.'

The landlord looked at me in return over the bar, from head to foot, with a strange smile on his face; and instead of drawing the beer, looked round the screen and said something to his wife. She came out from behind it, with her work in her hand, and joined him in surveying me. Here we stand, all three, before me now. The landlord in his shirt-sleeves, leaning against the bar window-frame; his wife looking over the little half-door; and I, in some confusion, looking up at them from outside the partition. They asked me a good many questions; as, what my name was, how old I was, where I lived, how I was employed, and how I came there. To all of which, that I might commit nobody, I invented, I am afraid, appropriate answers. They served me with the ale, though I suspect it was not the Genuine Stunning; and the landlord's wife, opening the little half-door of the bar, and bending down, gave me my money back, and gave me a kiss that was half admiring and half compassionate, but all womanly and good, I am sure.

I Make Myself Known To My Aunt

From Chapter XIII: "The Sequel Of My Resolution"

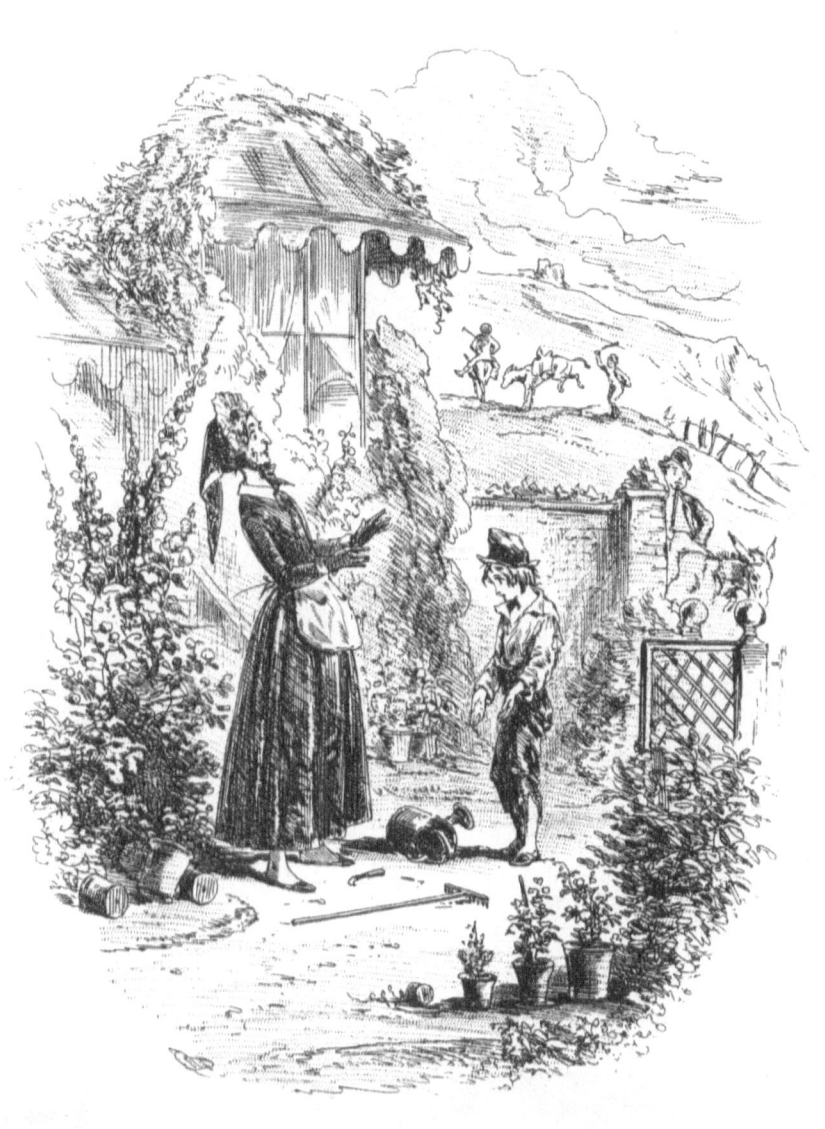

*M*y shoes were by this time in a woeful condition. The soles had shed themselves bit by bit, and the upper leathers had broken and burst until the very shape and form of shoes had departed from them. My hat (which had served me for a night-cap, too) was so crushed and bent, that no old battered handleless saucepan on a dunghill need have been ashamed to vie with it. My shirt and trousers, stained with heat, dew, grass, and the Kentish soil on which I had slept – and torn besides – might have frightened the birds from my aunt's garden, as I stood at the gate. My hair had known no comb or brush since I left London. My face, neck, and hands, from unaccustomed exposure to the air and sun, were burnt to a berry-brown. From head to foot I was powdered almost as white with chalk and dust, as if I had come out of a lime-kiln. In this plight, and with a strong consciousness of it, I waited to introduce myself to, and make my first impression on, my formidable aunt.

The unbroken stillness of the parlour window leading me to infer, after a while, that she was not there, I lifted up my eyes to the window above it, where I saw a florid, pleasant-looking gentleman, with a grey head, who shut up one eye in a grotesque manner, nodded his head at me several times, shook it at me as often, laughed, and went away.

I had been discomposed enough before; but I was so much the more discomposed by this unexpected behaviour, that I was on the point of slinking off, to think how I had best proceed, when there came out of the house a lady with her handkerchief tied over her cap, and a pair of gardening gloves on her hands, wearing a gardening pocket like a toll-man's apron, and carrying a great knife. I knew her immediately to be Miss Betsey, for she came stalking out of the house exactly as my poor mother had so often described her stalking up our garden at Blunderstone

Rookery.

'Go away!' said Miss Betsey, shaking her head, and making a distant chop in the air with her knife. 'Go along! No boys here!'

I watched her, with my heart at my lips, as she marched to a corner of her garden, and stooped to dig up some little root there. Then, without a scrap of courage, but with a great deal of desperation, I went softly in and stood beside her, touching her with my finger.

'If you please, ma'am,' I began.

She started and looked up.

'If you please, aunt.'

'EH?' exclaimed Miss Betsey, in a tone of amazement I have never heard approached.

'If you please, aunt, I am your nephew.'

'Oh, Lord!' said my aunt. And sat flat down in the garden-path.

'I am David Copperfield, of Blunderstone, in Suffolk – where you came, on the night when I was born, and saw my dear mama. I have been very unhappy since she died. I have been slighted, and taught nothing, and thrown upon myself, and put to work not fit for me. It made me run away to you. I was robbed at first setting out, and have walked all the way, and have never slept in a bed since I began the journey.' Here my self-support gave way all at once; and with a movement of my hands, intended to show her my ragged state, and call it to witness that I had suffered something, I broke into a passion of crying, which I suppose had been pent up within me all the week.

My aunt, with every sort of expression but wonder discharged from her countenance, sat on the gravel, staring at me, until I began to cry; when she got up in a great hurry, collared me, and took me into the parlour. Her first proceeding there was to unlock a tall press, bring out several bottles, and pour some of the contents of each into my mouth. I think they must have been taken out at random, for I am sure I tasted aniseed water, anchovy sauce, and salad dressing. When she had administered these restoratives, as I was still quite hysterical, and unable to control my sobs, she put me on the sofa, with a shawl under my head, and the handkerchief from her own head under my feet, lest I should sully the cover; and then, sitting herself down behind the green fan or screen I have already mentioned, so that I could not see her face, ejaculated at intervals, 'Mercy on us!' letting those exclamations off like minute guns.

The Momentous Interview

From Chapter XIV: "My Aunt Makes Up Her Mind About Me"

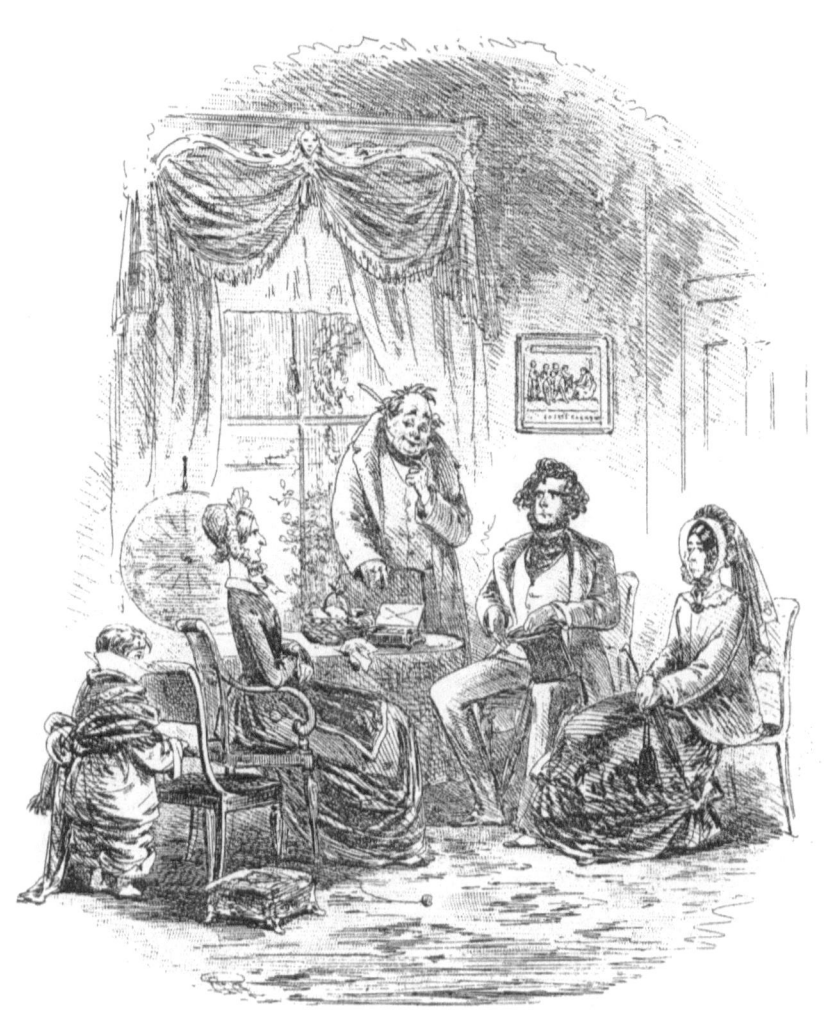

*S*hall I go away, aunt?' I asked, trembling.

'No, sir,' said my aunt. 'Certainly not!' With which she pushed me into a corner near her, and fenced me in with a chair, as if it were a prison or a bar of justice. This position I continued to occupy during the whole interview, and from it I now saw Mr. and Miss Murdstone enter the room.

'Oh!' said my aunt, 'I was not aware at first to whom I had the pleasure of objecting. But I don't allow anybody to ride over that turf. I make no exceptions. I don't allow anybody to do it.'

'Your regulation is rather awkward to strangers,' said Miss Murdstone.

'Is it!' said my aunt.

Mr. Murdstone seemed afraid of a renewal of hostilities, and interposing began:

'Miss Trotwood!'

'I beg your pardon,' observed my aunt with a keen look. 'You are the Mr. Murdstone who married the widow of my late nephew, David Copperfield, of Blunderstone Rookery! – Though why Rookery, I don't know!'

'I am,' said Mr. Murdstone.

'You'll excuse my saying, sir,' returned my aunt, 'that I think it would have been a much better and happier thing if you had left that poor child alone.'

'I so far agree with what Miss Trotwood has remarked,' observed Miss Murdstone, bridling, 'that I consider our lamented Clara to have been, in all essential respects, a mere child.'

'It is a comfort to you and me, ma'am,' said my aunt, 'who are getting on in life, and are not likely to be made unhappy by our personal attractions, that nobody can say the same of us.'

'No doubt!' returned Miss Murdstone, though, I thought, not with a very ready or gracious assent. 'And it certainly might have been, as you say, a better and happier thing for my brother if he had never entered into such a marriage. I have always been of that opinion.'

'I have no doubt you have,' said my aunt. 'Janet,' ringing the bell, 'my compliments to Mr. Dick, and beg him to come down.'

Until he came, my aunt sat perfectly upright and stiff, frowning at the wall. When he came, my aunt performed the ceremony of introduction.

'Mr. Dick. An old and intimate friend. On whose judgement,' said my aunt, with emphasis, as an admonition to Mr. Dick, who was biting his forefinger and looking rather foolish, 'I rely.'

Mr. Dick took his finger out of his mouth, on this hint, and stood among the group, with a grave and attentive expression of face.

My aunt inclined her head to Mr. Murdstone, who went on:

'Miss Trotwood: on the receipt of your letter, I considered it an act of greater justice to myself, and perhaps of more respect to you-'

'Thank you,' said my aunt, still eyeing him keenly. 'You needn't mind me.'

'To answer it in person, however inconvenient the journey,' pursued Mr. Murdstone, 'rather than by letter. This unhappy boy who has run away from his friends and his occupation -'

'And whose appearance,' interposed his sister, directing general attention to me in my indefinable costume, 'is perfectly *scandalous and disgraceful.'*

'Jane Murdstone,' said her brother, 'have the goodness not to interrupt me. This unhappy boy, Miss Trotwood, has been the occasion of much domestic trouble and uneasiness; both during the lifetime of my late dear wife, and since. He has a sullen, rebellious spirit; a violent temper; and an untoward, intractable disposition. Both my sister and myself have endeavoured to correct his vices, but ineffectually. And I have felt — we both have felt, I may say; my sister being fully in my confidence — that it is right you should receive this grave and dispassionate assurance from our lips.'

'It can hardly be necessary for me to confirm anything stated by my brother,' said Miss Murdstone; 'but I beg to observe, that, of all the boys in the world, I believe this is the worst boy.'

'Strong!' said my aunt, shortly.

'But not at all too strong for the facts,' returned Miss Murdstone.

'Ha!' said my aunt. 'Well, sir?'

'I have my own opinions,' resumed Mr. Murdstone, whose face darkened more and more, the more he and my aunt observed each other, which they did very narrowly, 'as to the best mode of bringing him up; they are founded, in part, on my knowledge of him, and in part on my knowledge of my own means and resources. I am responsible for them to myself, I act upon them, and I say no more about them. It is enough that I place this boy under the eye of a friend of my own, in a respectable business; that it does not please him; that he runs away from it; makes himself a common vagabond about the country; and comes here, in rags, to appeal to you, Miss Trotwood. I wish to set before you, honourably, the exact consequences — so far as they are within my knowledge — of your abetting him in this

appeal.'

'But about the respectable business first,' said my aunt. 'If he had been your own boy, you would have put him to it, just the same, I suppose?'

'If he had been my brother's own boy,' returned Miss Murdstone, striking in, 'his character, I trust, would have been altogether different.'

'Or if the poor child, his mother, had been alive, he would still have gone into the respectable business, would he?' said my aunt.

'I believe,' said Mr. Murdstone, with an inclination of his head, 'that Clara would have disputed nothing which myself and my sister Jane Murdstone were agreed was for the best.'

Miss Murdstone confirmed this with an audible murmur.

'Humph!' said my aunt. 'Unfortunate baby!'

Mr. Dick, who had been rattling his money all this time, was rattling it so loudly now, that my aunt felt it necessary to check him with a look, before saying:

'The poor child's annuity died with her?'

'Died with her,' replied Mr. Murdstone.

'And there was no settlement of the little property — the house and garden — the what's-its-name Rookery without any rooks in it — upon her boy?'

'It had been left to her, unconditionally, by her first husband,' Mr. Murdstone began, when my aunt caught him up with the greatest irascibility and impatience.

'Good Lord, man, there's no occasion to say that. Left to her unconditionally! I think I see David Copperfield looking forward to any condition of any sort or kind, though it stared him point-blank in the face! Of course it was left to her uncondition-

ally. But when she married again – when she took that most disastrous step of marrying you, in short,' said my aunt, 'to be plain – did no one put in a word for the boy at that time?'

'My late wife loved her second husband, ma'am,' said Mr. Murdstone, 'and trusted implicitly in him.'

'Your late wife, sir, was a most unworldly, most unhappy, most unfortunate baby,' returned my aunt, shaking her head at him. 'That's what she was. And now, what have you got to say next?'

'Merely this, Miss Trotwood,' he returned. 'I am here to take David back – to take him back unconditionally, to dispose of him as I think proper, and to deal with him as I think right. I am not here to make any promise, or give any pledge to anybody. You may possibly have some idea, Miss Trotwood, of abetting him in his running away, and in his complaints to you. Your manner, which I must say does not seem intended to propitiate, induces me to think it possible. Now I must caution you that if you abet him once, you abet him for good and all; if you step in between him and me, now, you must step in, Miss Trotwood, for ever. I cannot trifle, or be trifled with. I am here, for the first and last time, to take him away. Is he ready to go? If he is not – and you tell me he is not; on any pretence; it is indifferent to me what – my doors are shut against him henceforth, and yours, I take it for granted, are open to him.'

To this address, my aunt had listened with the closest attention, sitting perfectly upright, with her hands folded on one knee, and looking grimly on the speaker. When he had finished, she turned her eyes so as to command Miss Murdstone, without otherwise disturbing her attitude, and said:

'Well, ma'am, have YOU got anything to remark?'

'Indeed, Miss Trotwood,' said Miss Murdstone, 'all that I

could say has been so well said by my brother, and all that I know to be the fact has been so plainly stated by him, that I have nothing to add except my thanks for your politeness. For your very great politeness, I am sure,' said Miss Murdstone; with an irony which no more affected my aunt, than it discomposed the cannon I had slept by at Chatham.

'And what does the boy say?' said my aunt. 'Are you ready to go, David?'

I answered no, and entreated her not to let me go. I said that neither Mr. nor Miss Murdstone had ever liked me, or had ever been kind to me. That they had made my mama, who always loved me dearly, unhappy about me, and that I knew it well, and that Peggotty knew it. I said that I had been more miserable than I thought anybody could believe, who only knew how young I was. And I begged and prayed my aunt – I forget in what terms now, but I remember that they affected me very much then – to befriend and protect me, for my father's sake.

'Mr. Dick,' said my aunt, 'what shall I do with this child?'

Mr. Dick considered, hesitated, brightened, and rejoined, 'Have him measured for a suit of clothes directly.'

'Mr. Dick,' said my aunt triumphantly, 'give me your hand, for your common sense is invaluable.' Having shaken it with great cordiality, she pulled me towards her and said to Mr. Murdstone:

'You can go when you like; I'll take my chance with the boy. If he's all you say he is, at least I can do as much for him then, as you have done. But I don't believe a word of it.'

'Miss Trotwood,' rejoined Mr. Murdstone, shrugging his shoulders, as he rose, 'if you were a gentleman -'

'Bah! Stuff and nonsense!' said my aunt. 'Don't talk to me!'

'How exquisitely polite!' exclaimed Miss Murdstone, rising. 'Overpowering, really!'

'Do you think I don't know,' said my aunt, turning a deaf ear to the sister, and continuing to address the brother, and to shake her head at him with infinite expression, 'what kind of life you must have led that poor, unhappy, misdirected baby? Do you think I don't know what a woeful day it was for the soft little creature when you first came in her way — smirking and making great eyes at her, I'll be bound, as if you couldn't say boh! to a goose!'

'I never heard anything so elegant!' said Miss Murdstone.

'Do you think I can't understand you as well as if I had seen you,' pursued my aunt, 'now that I DO see and hear you — which, I tell you candidly, is anything but a pleasure to me? Oh yes, bless us! who so smooth and silky as Mr. Murdstone at first! The poor, benighted innocent had never seen such a man. He was made of sweetness. He worshipped her. He doted on her boy — tenderly doted on him! He was to be another father to him, and they were all to live together in a garden of roses, weren't they? Ugh! Get along with you, do!' said my aunt.

'I never heard anything like this person in my life!' exclaimed Miss Murdstone.

'And when you had made sure of the poor little fool,' said my aunt — 'God forgive me that I should call her so, and she gone where YOU won't go in a hurry — because you had not done wrong enough to her and hers, you must begin to train her, must you? begin to break her, like a poor caged bird, and wear her deluded life away, in teaching her to sing YOUR notes?'

'This is either insanity or intoxication,' said Miss Murdstone, in a perfect agony at not being able to turn the current of my aunt's address towards herself; 'and my suspicion is

105

that it's intoxication.'

Miss Betsey, without taking the least notice of the interruption, continued to address herself to Mr. Murdstone as if there had been no such thing.

'Mr. Murdstone,' she said, shaking her finger at him, 'you were a tyrant to the simple baby, and you broke her heart. She was a loving baby – I know that; I knew it, years before you ever saw her – and through the best part of her weakness you gave her the wounds she died of. There is the truth for your comfort, however you like it. And you and your instruments may make the most of it.'

'Allow me to inquire, Miss Trotwood,' interposed Miss Murdstone, 'whom you are pleased to call, in a choice of words in which I am not experienced, my brother's instruments?'

'It was clear enough, as I have told you, years before YOU ever saw her – and why, in the mysterious dispensations of Providence, you ever did see her, is more than humanity can comprehend – it was clear enough that the poor soft little thing would marry somebody, at some time or other; but I did hope it wouldn't have been as bad as it has turned out. That was the time, Mr. Murdstone, when she gave birth to her boy here,' said my aunt; 'to the poor child you sometimes tormented her through afterwards, which is a disagreeable remembrance and makes the sight of him odious now. Aye, aye! you needn't wince!' said my aunt. 'I know it's true without that.'

He had stood by the door, all this while, observant of her with a smile upon his face, though his black eyebrows were heavily contracted. I remarked now, that, though the smile was on his face still, his colour had gone in a moment, and he seemed to breathe as if he had been running.

'Good day, sir,' said my aunt, 'and good-bye! Good day to

you, too, ma'am,' said my aunt, turning suddenly upon his sister. 'Let me see you ride a donkey over my green again, and as sure as you have a head upon your shoulders, I'll knock your bonnet off, and tread upon it!'

I Return To The Doctor's After The Party

From Chapter XVI: "I Am A New Boy In More Senses Than One"

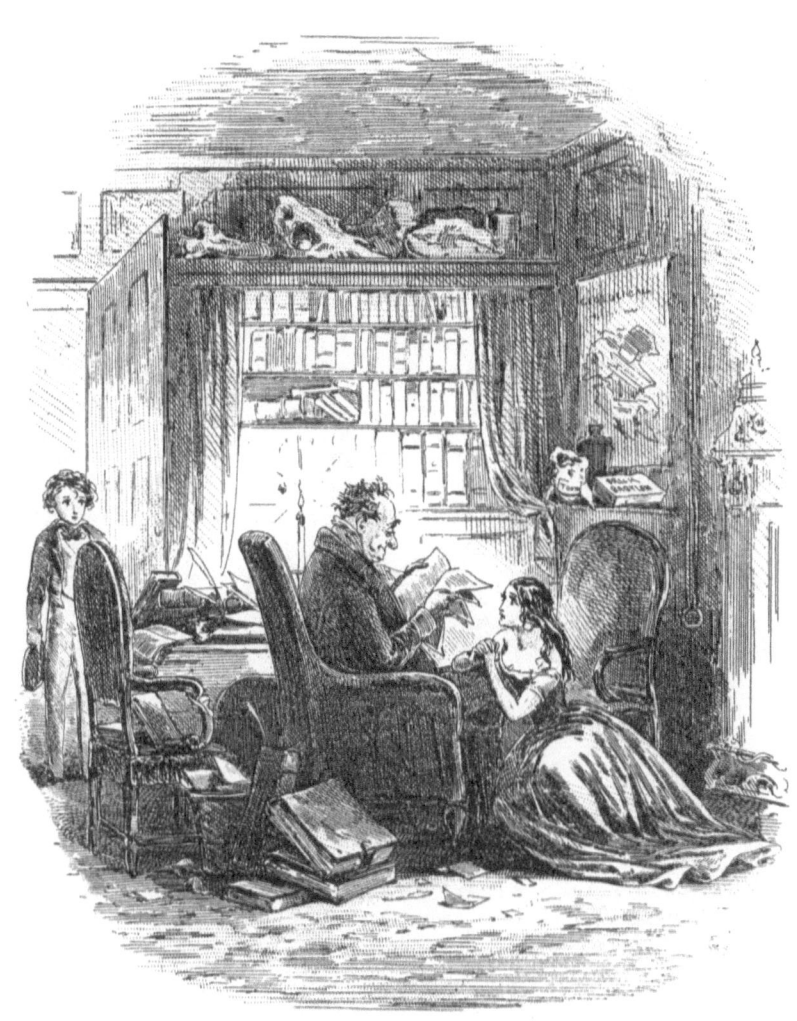

*W*hen we, at last, reached our own door, Agnes discovered that she had left her little reticule behind. Delighted to be of any service to her, I ran back to fetch it.

I went into the supper-room where it had been left, which was deserted and dark. But a door of communication between that and the Doctor's study, where there was a light, being open, I passed on there, to say what I wanted, and to get a candle.

The Doctor was sitting in his easy-chair by the fireside, and his young wife was on a stool at his feet. The Doctor, with a complacent smile, was reading aloud some manuscript explanation or statement of a theory out of that interminable Dictionary, and she was looking up at him. But with such a face as I never saw. It was so beautiful in its form, it was so ashy pale, it was so fixed in its abstraction, it was so full of a wild, sleep-walking, dreamy horror of I don't know what. The eyes were wide open, and her brown hair fell in two rich clusters on her shoulders, and on her white dress, disordered by the want of the lost ribbon. Distinctly as I recollect her look, I cannot say of what it was expressive, I cannot even say of what it is expressive to me now, rising again before my older judgement. Penitence, humiliation, shame, pride, love, and trustfulness — I see them all; and in them all, I see that horror of I don't know what.

My entrance, and my saying what I wanted, roused her. It disturbed the Doctor too, for when I went back to replace the candle I had taken from the table, he was patting her head, in his fatherly way, and saying he was a merciless drone to let her tempt him into reading on; and he would have her go to bed.

But she asked him, in a rapid, urgent manner, to let her stay — to let her feel assured (I heard her murmur some broken words to this effect) that she was in his confidence that night. And, as *she turned again towards him, after glancing at me as I left the room and went out at the door, I saw her cross her hands upon his knee, and look up at him with the same face, something quieted, as he resumed his reading.*

It made a great impression on me, and I remembered it a long time afterwards; as I shall have occasion to narrate when the time comes.

Somebody Turns Up

From Chapter XVII: "Somebody Turns Up"

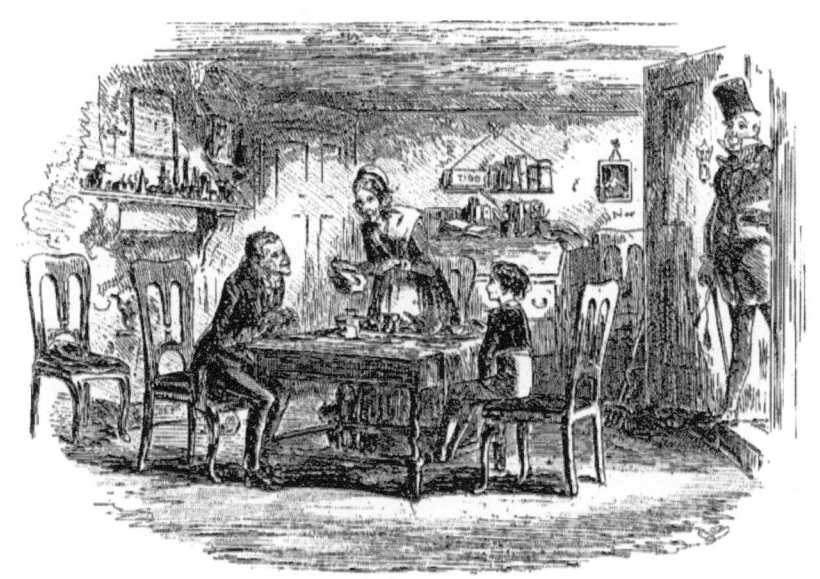

I had begun to be a little uncomfortable, and to wish myself well out of the visit, when a figure coming down the street passed the door – it stood open to air the room, which was warm, the weather being close for the time of year – came back again, looked in, and walked in, exclaiming loudly, 'Copperfield! Is it possible?'

It was Mr. Micawber! It was Mr. Micawber, with his eyeglass, and his walking-stick, and his shirt-collar, and his genteel air, and the condescending roll in his voice, all complete!

'My dear Copperfield,' said Mr. Micawber, putting out his hand, 'this is indeed a meeting which is calculated to impress the mind with a sense of the instability and uncertainty of all human – in short, it is a most extraordinary meeting. Walking along the street, reflecting upon the probability of something turning up (of which I am at present rather sanguine), I find a young but valued friend turn up, who is connected with the most eventful period of my life; I may say, with the turning-point of my existence. Copperfield, my dear fellow, how do you do?'

I cannot say – I really cannot say – that I was glad to see Mr. Micawber there; but I was glad to see him too, and shook hands with him, heartily, inquiring how Mrs. Micawber was.

My First Fall In Life

From Chapter XIX: "I Look About Me And Make A Discovery"

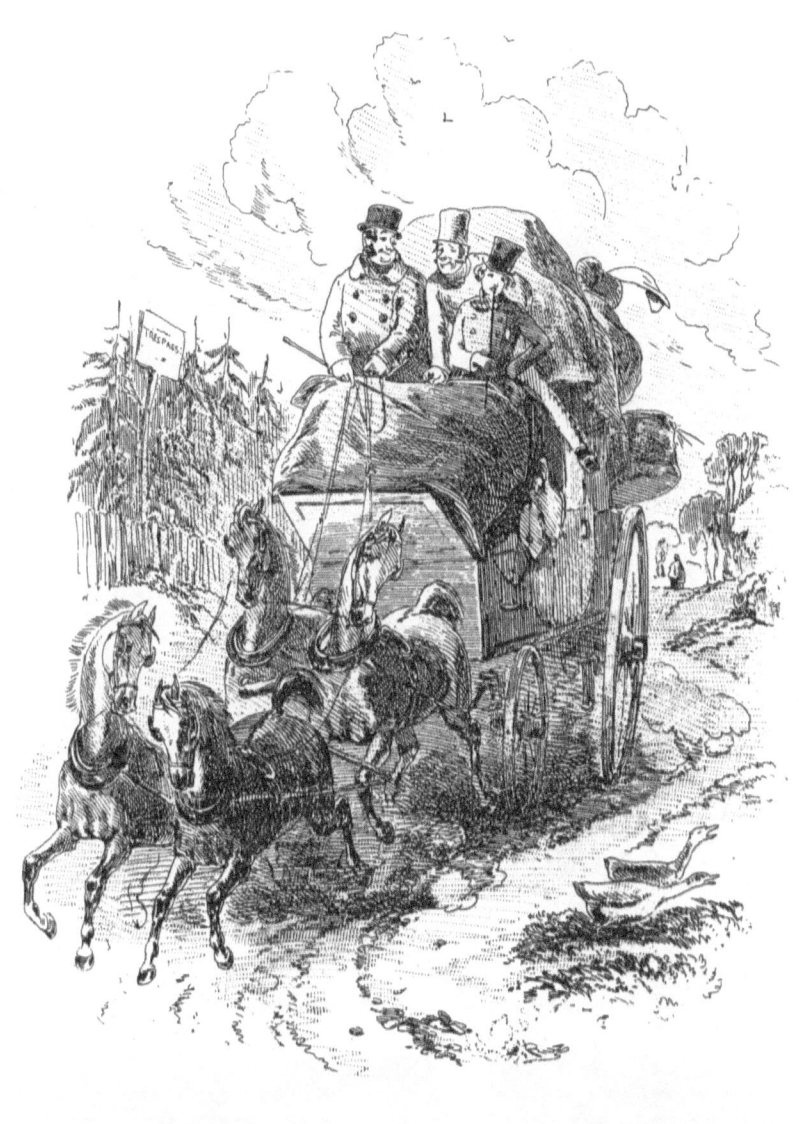

*7*hat ain't a sort of man to see sitting behind a coach-box, is it though?' said William in my ear, as he handled the reins.

I construed this remark into an indication of a wish that he should have my place, so I blushingly offered to resign it.

'Well, if you don't mind, sir,' said William, 'I think it would be more correct.'

I have always considered this as the first fall I had in life. When I booked my place at the coach office I had had 'Box Seat' written against the entry, and had given the book-keeper half-a-crown. I was got up in a special great-coat and shawl, expressly to do honour to that distinguished eminence; had glorified myself upon it a good deal; and had felt that I was a credit to the coach. And here, in the very first stage, I was supplanted by a shabby man with a squint, who had no other merit than smelling like a livery-stables, and being able to walk across me, more like a fly than a human being, while the horses were at a canter!

A distrust of myself, which has often beset me in life on small occasions, when it would have been better away, was assuredly not stopped in its growth by this little incident outside the Canterbury coach. It was in vain to take refuge in gruffness of speech. I spoke from the pit of my stomach for the rest of the journey, but I felt completely extinguished, and dreadfully young.

It was curious and interesting, nevertheless, to be sitting up there behind four horses: well educated, well dressed, and with plenty of money in my pocket; and to look out for the places where I had slept on my weary journey. I had abundant occupation for my thoughts, in every conspicuous landmark on the road. When I looked down at the trampers whom we passed, and saw that well-remembered style of face turned up, I felt as if the tinker's blackened hand were in the bosom of my shirt again. When we clattered through the narrow street of Chatham, and I caught a glimpse, in passing, of the lane where the old monster lived who had bought my jacket, I stretched my neck eagerly to look for the place where I had sat, in the sun and in the shade, waiting for my money. When we came, at last, within a stage of London, and passed the veritable Salem House where Mr. Creakle had laid about him with a heavy hand, I would have given all I had, for lawful permission to get down and thrash him, and let all the boys out like so many caged sparrows.

We Arrive Unexpectedly At Mr. Peggotty's Fireside

From Chapter XXI: "Little Em'ly"

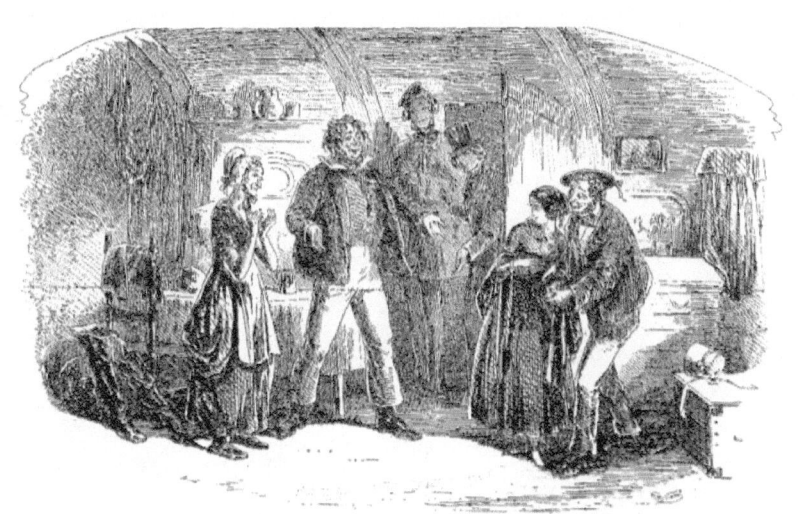

*7*his is a wild kind of place, Steerforth, is it not?'

'Dismal enough in the dark,' he said: 'and the sea roars as if it were hungry for us. Is that the boat, where I see a light yonder?' 'That's the boat,' said I.

'And it's the same I saw this morning,' he returned. 'I came straight to it, by instinct, I suppose.'

We said no more as we approached the light, but made softly for the door. I laid my hand upon the latch; and whispering Steerforth to keep close to me, went in.

A murmur of voices had been audible on the outside, and, at the moment of our entrance, a clapping of hands: which latter noise, I was surprised to see, proceeded from the generally disconsolate Mrs. Gummidge. But Mrs. Gummidge was not the only person there who was unusually excited. Mr. Peggotty, his face lighted up with uncommon satisfaction, and laughing with all his might, held his rough arms wide open, as if for little Em'ly to run into them; Ham, with a mixed expression in his face of admiration, exultation, and a lumbering sort of bashfulness that sat upon him very well, held little Em'ly by the hand, as if he were presenting her to Mr. Peggotty; little Em'ly herself, blushing and shy, but delighted with Mr. Peggotty's delight, as her joyous eyes expressed, was stopped by our entrance (for she saw us first) in the very act of springing from Ham to nestle in Mr. Peggotty's embrace. In the first glimpse we had of them all, and at the moment of our passing from the dark cold night into the warm light room, this was the way in which they were all employed: Mrs. Gummidge in the background, clapping her hands like a madwoman.

The little picture was so instantaneously dissolved by our going in, that one might have doubted whether it had ever been. I was in the midst of the astonished family, face to face with Mr.

Peggotty, and holding out my hand to him, when Ham shouted:

'Mas'r Davy! It's Mas'r Davy!'

In a moment we were all shaking hands with one another, and asking one another how we did, and telling one another how glad we were to meet, and all talking at once. Mr. Peggotty was so proud and overjoyed to see us, that he did not know what to say or do, but kept over and over again shaking hands with me, and then with Steerforth, and then with me, and then ruffling his shaggy hair all over his head, and laughing with such glee and triumph, that it was a treat to see him.

I Make The Acquaintance Of Miss Mowcher

From Chapter XXII: "Some Old Scenes, And Some New People"

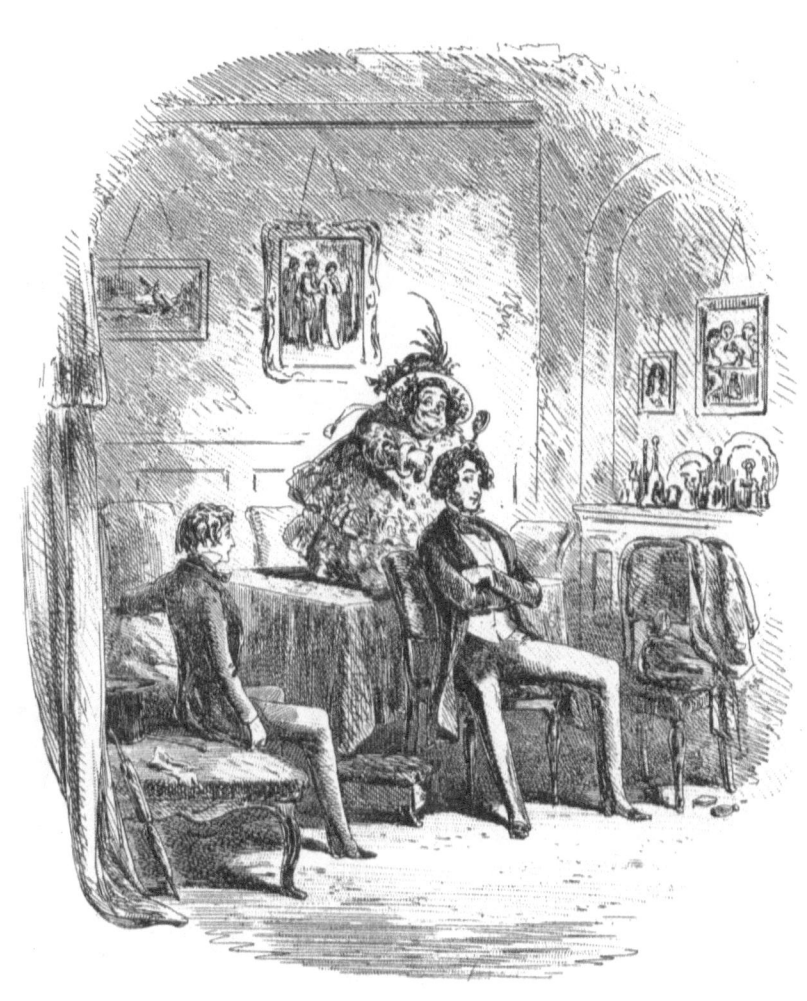

I looked at the doorway and saw nothing. I was still looking at the doorway, thinking that Miss Mowcher was a long while making her appearance, when, to my infinite astonishment, there came waddling round a sofa which stood between me and it, a pursy dwarf, of about forty or forty-five, with a very large head and face, a pair of roguish grey eyes, and such extremely little arms, that, to enable herself to lay a finger archly against her snub nose, as she ogled Steerforth, she was obliged to meet the finger half-way, and lay her nose against it. Her chin, which was what is called a double chin, was so fat that it entirely swallowed up the strings of her bonnet, bow and all. Throat she had none; waist she had none; legs she had none, worth mentioning; for though she was more than full-sized down to where her waist would have been, if she had had any, and though she terminated, as human beings generally do, in a pair of feet, she was so short that she stood at a common-sized chair as at a table, resting a bag she carried on the seat. This lady – dressed in an off-hand, easy style; bringing her nose and her forefinger together, with the difficulty I have described; standing with her head necessarily on one side, and, with one of her sharp eyes shut up, making an uncommonly knowing face – after ogling Steerforth for a few moments, broke into a torrent of words.

Martha

From Chapter XXII: "Some Old Scenes, And Some New People"

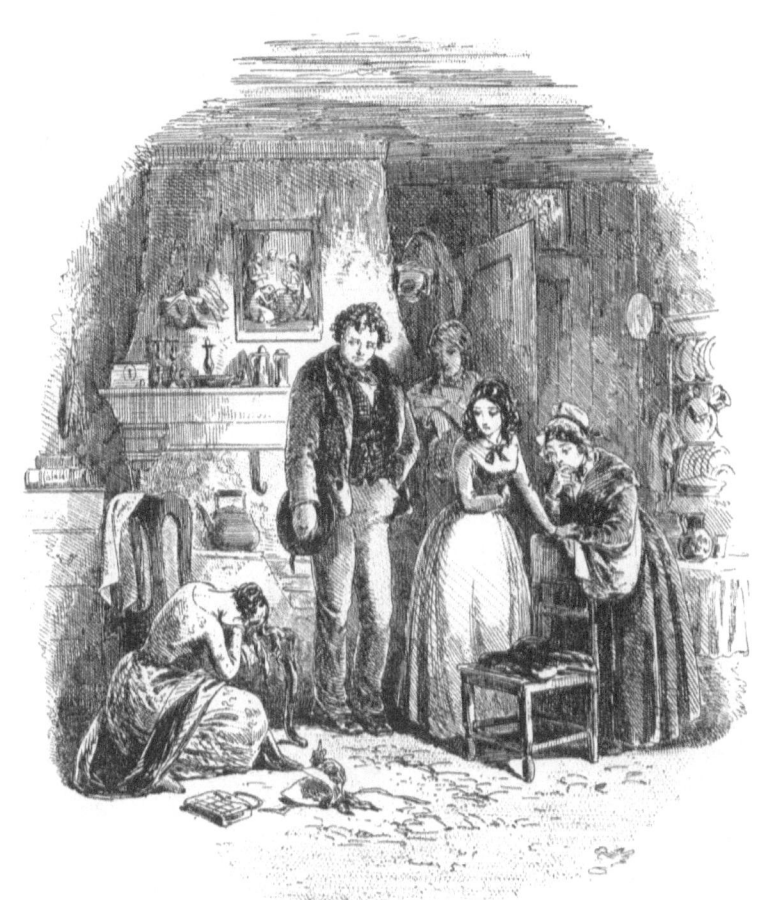

*7*he girl – the same I had seen upon the sands – was near the fire. She was sitting on the ground, with her head and one arm lying on a chair. I fancied, from the disposition of her figure, that Em'ly had but newly risen from the chair, and that the forlorn head might perhaps have been lying on her lap. I saw but little of the girl's face, over which her hair fell loose and scattered, as if she had been disordering it with her own hands; but I saw that she was young, and of a fair complexion. Peggotty had been crying. So had little Em'ly. Not a word was spoken when we first went in; and the Dutch clock by the dresser seemed, in the silence, to tick twice as loud as usual. Em'ly spoke first.

'Martha wants,' she said to Ham, 'to go to London.'

'Why to London?' returned Ham.

He stood between them, looking on the prostrate girl with a mixture of compassion for her, and of jealousy of her holding any companionship with her whom he loved so well, which I have always remembered distinctly. They both spoke as if she were ill; in a soft, suppressed tone that was plainly heard, although it hardly rose above a whisper.

'Better there than here,' said a third voice aloud – Martha's, though she did not move. 'No one knows me there. Everybody knows me here.'

'What will she do there?' inquired Ham.

She lifted up her head, and looked darkly round at him for a moment; then laid it down again, and curved her right arm about her neck, as a woman in a fever, or in an agony of pain from a shot, might twist herself.

'She will try to do well,' said little Em'ly. 'You don't know what she has said to us. Does he – do they – aunt?'

Peggotty shook her head compassionately.

'I'll try,' said Martha, 'if you'll help me away. I never can do worse than I have done here. I may do better. Oh!' with a dreadful shiver, 'take me out of these streets, where the whole town knows me from a child!'

As Em'ly held out her hand to Ham, I saw him put in it a little canvas bag. She took it, as if she thought it were her purse, and made a step or two forward; but finding her mistake, came back to where he had retired near me, and showed it to him.

'It's all yourn, Em'ly,' I could hear him say. 'I haven't nowt in all the wureld that ain't yourn, my dear. It ain't of no delight to me, except for you!'

The tears rose freshly in her eyes, but she turned away and went to Martha. What she gave her, I don't know. I saw her stooping over her, and putting money in her bosom. She whispered something, as she asked was that enough? 'More than enough,' the other said, and took her hand and kissed it.

Then Martha arose, and gathering her shawl about her, covering her face with it, and weeping aloud, went slowly to the door. She stopped a moment before going out, as if she would have uttered something or turned back; but no word passed her lips. Making the same low, dreary, wretched moaning in her shawl, she went away.

Uriah Persists In Hovering Near Us, At The Dinner-Party

From Chapter XXV: "Good And Bad Angels"

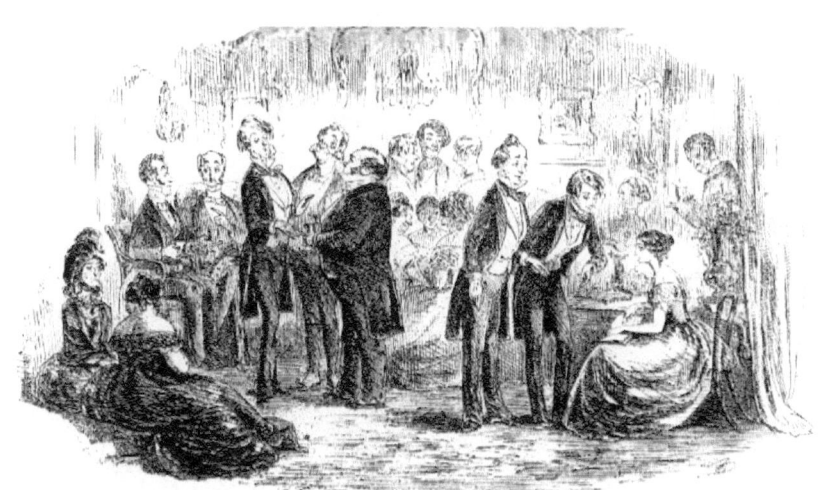

*W*hen I went to dinner next day, and on the street door being opened, plunged into a vapour-bath of haunch of mutton, I divined that I was not the only guest, for I immediately identified the ticket-porter in disguise, assisting the family servant, and waiting at the foot of the stairs to carry up my name. He looked, to the best of his ability, when he asked me for it confidentially, as if he had never seen me before; but well did I know him, and well did he know me. Conscience made cowards of us both.

I found Mr. Waterbrook to be a middle-aged gentleman, with a short throat, and a good deal of shirt-collar, who only wanted a black nose to be the portrait of a pug-dog. He told me he was happy to have the honour of making my acquaintance; and when I had paid my homage to Mrs. Waterbrook, presented me, with much ceremony, to a very awful lady in a black velvet dress, and a great black velvet hat, whom I remember as looking like a near relation of Hamlet's – say his aunt.

Mrs. Henry Spiker was this lady's name; and her husband was there too: so cold a man, that his head, instead of being grey, seemed to be sprinkled with hoar-frost. Immense deference was shown to the Henry Spikers, male and female; which Agnes told me was on account of Mr. Henry Spiker being solicitor to something Or to Somebody, I forget what or which, remotely connected with the Treasury.

I found Uriah Heep among the company, in a suit of black, and in deep humility. He told me, when I shook hands with him, that he was proud to be noticed by me, and that he really felt obliged to me for my condescension. I could have wished he had been less obliged to me, for he hovered about me in his gratitude all the rest of the evening; and whenever I said a word to Agnes, was sure, with his shadowless eyes and cadaverous face, to *be looking gauntly down upon us from behind.*

I Fall Into Captivity

From Chapter XXVI: "I Fall Into Captivity"

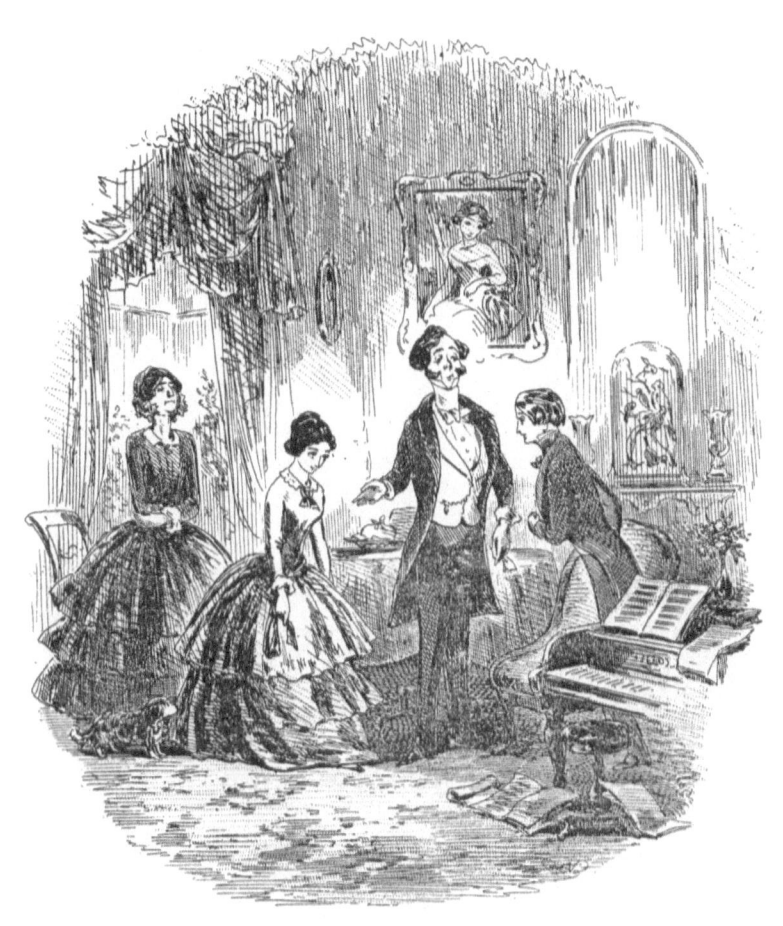

We went into the house, which was cheerfully lighted up, and into a hall where there were all sorts of hats, caps, great-coats, plaids, gloves, whips, and walking-sticks. 'Where is Miss Dora?' said Mr. Spenlow to the servant. 'Dora!' I thought. 'What a beautiful name!'

We turned into a room near at hand (I think it was the identical breakfast-room, made memorable by the brown East Indian sherry), and I heard a voice say, 'Mr. Copperfield, my daughter Dora, and my daughter Dora's confidential friend!' It was, no doubt, Mr. Spenlow's voice, but I didn't know it, and I didn't care whose it was. All was over in a moment. I had fulfilled my destiny. I was a captive and a slave. I loved Dora Spenlow to distraction!

She was more than human to me. She was a Fairy, a Sylph, I don't know what she was — anything that no one ever saw, and everything that everybody ever wanted. I was swallowed up in an abyss of love in an instant. There was no pausing on the brink; no looking down, or looking back; I was gone, headlong, before I had sense to say a word to her.

We Are Disturbed In Our Cookery

From Chapter XXVIII: "Mr. Micawber's Gauntlet"

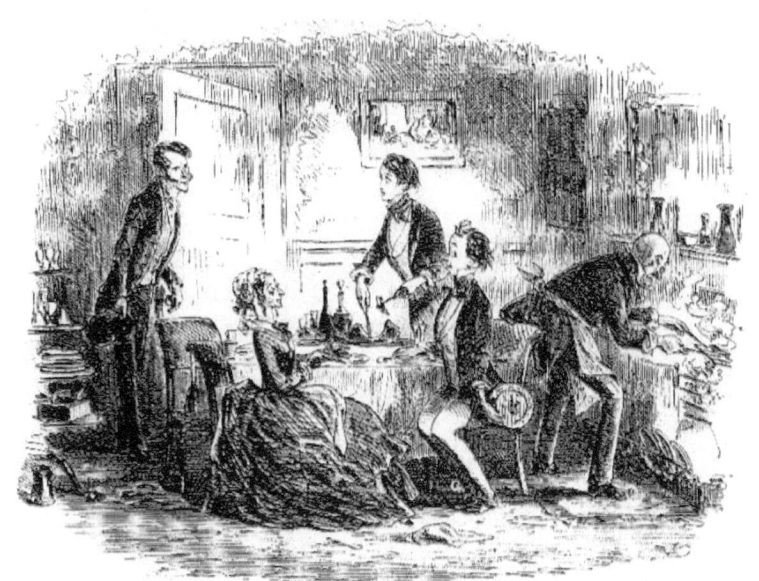

*W*hat with the novelty of this cookery, the excellence of it, the bustle of it, the frequent starting up to look after it, the frequent sitting down to dispose of it as the crisp slices came off the gridiron hot and hot, the being so busy, so flushed with the fire, so amused, and in the midst of such a tempting noise and savour, we reduced the leg of mutton to the bone. My own appetite came back miraculously. I am ashamed to record it, but I really believe I forgot Dora for a little while. I am satisfied that Mr. and Mrs. Micawber could not have enjoyed the feast more, if they had sold a bed to provide it. Traddles laughed as heartily, almost the whole time, as he ate and worked. Indeed we all did, all at once; and I dare say there was never a greater success.

We were at the height of our enjoyment, and were all busily engaged, in our several departments, endeavouring to bring the last batch of slices to a state of perfection that should crown the feast, when I was aware of a strange presence in the room, and my eyes encountered those of the staid Littimer, standing hat in hand before me.

'What's the matter?' I involuntarily asked.

'I beg your pardon, sir, I was directed to come in. Is my master not here, sir?'

'No.'

'Have you not seen him, sir?'

'No; don't you come from him?'

'Not immediately so, sir.'

'Did he tell you you would find him here?'

'Not exactly so, sir. But I should think he might be here tomorrow, as he has not been here today.' 'Is he coming up from Oxford?'

'I beg, sir,' he returned respectfully, 'that you will be seated, and allow me to do this.' With which he took the fork from my unresisting hand, and bent over the gridiron, as if his whole attention were concentrated on it.

I Find Mr. Barkis Going Out With The Tide

From Chapter XXX: "A Loss"

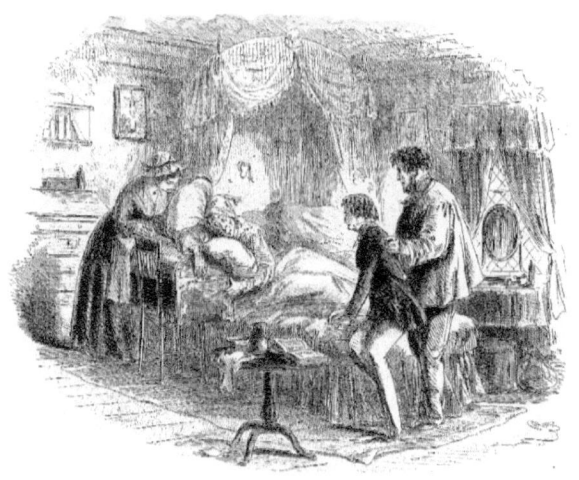

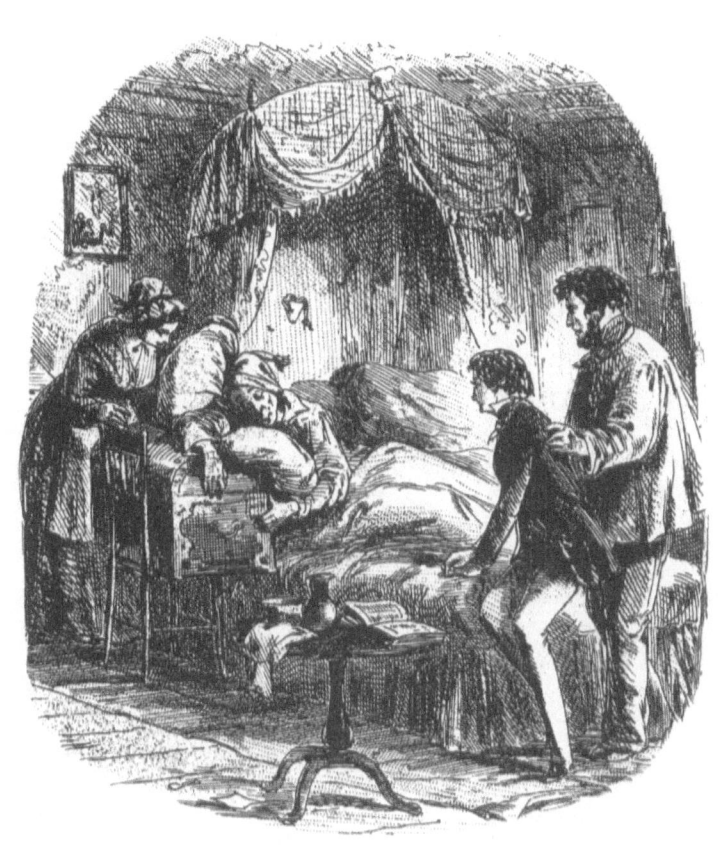

*B*arkis, my dear!' said Peggotty, almost cheerfully: bending over him, while her brother and I stood at the bed's foot. 'Here's my dear boy — my dear boy, Master Davy, who brought us together, Barkis! That you sent messages by, you know! Won't you speak to Master Davy?'

He was as mute and senseless as the box, from which his form derived the only expression it had.

'He's a going out with the tide,' said Mr. Peggotty to me, behind his hand.

My eyes were dim and so were Mr. Peggotty's; but I repeated in a whisper, 'With the tide?'

'People can't die, along the coast,' said Mr. Peggotty, 'except when the tide's pretty nigh out. They can't be born, unless it's pretty nigh in — not properly born, till flood. He's a going out with the tide. It's ebb at half-arter three, slack water half an hour. If he lives till it turns, he'll hold his own till past the flood, and go out with the next tide.'

We remained there, watching him, a long time — hours. What mysterious influence my presence had upon him in that state of his senses, I shall not pretend to say; but when he at last began to wander feebly, it is certain he was muttering about driving me to school.

'He's coming to himself,' said Peggotty.

Mr. Peggotty touched me, and whispered with much awe and reverence. 'They are both a-going out fast.'

'Barkis, my dear!' said Peggotty.

'C. P. Barkis,' he cried faintly. 'No better woman any-where!'

'Look! Here's Master Davy!' said Peggotty. For he now opened his eyes.

I was on the point of asking him if he knew me, when he tried to stretch out his arm, and said to me, distinctly, with a pleasant smile:

'Barkis is willin'!'

And, it being low water, he went out with the tide.

Mr. Peggotty And Mrs. Steerforth

From Chapter XXXII: "The Beginning Of A Long Journey"

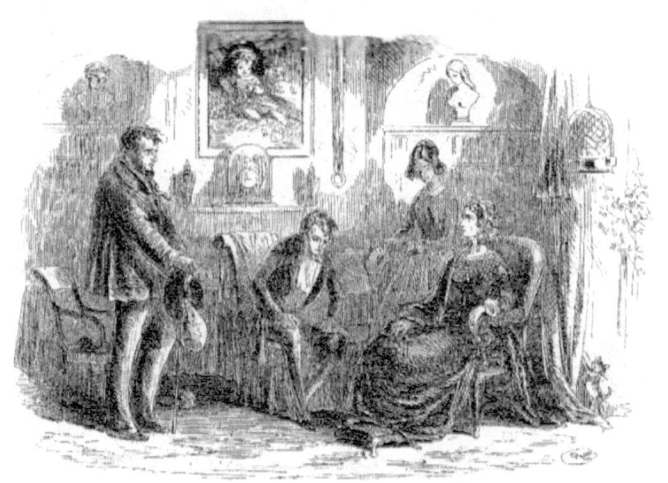

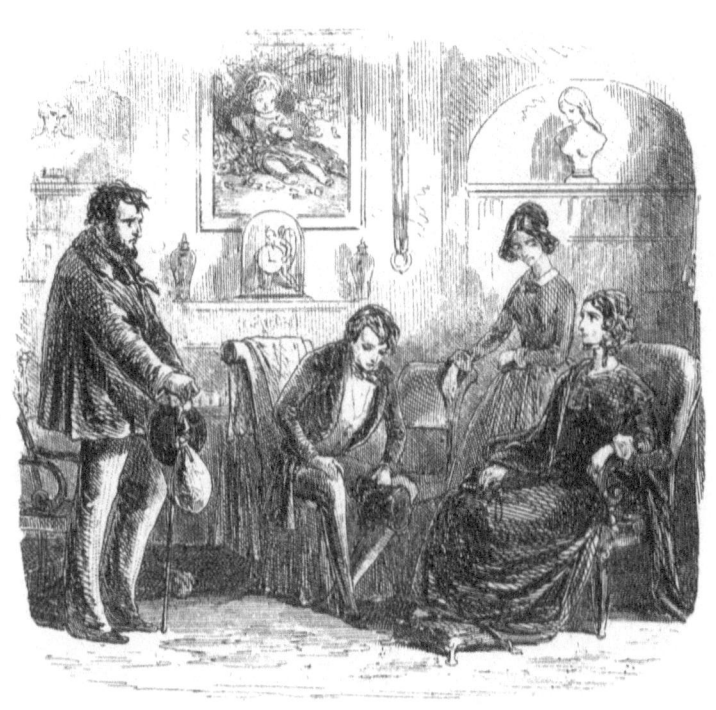

I saw, *directly*, *in his mother's face, that she knew from himself what he had done. It was very pale; and bore the traces of deeper emotion than my letter alone, weakened by the doubts her fondness would have raised upon it, would have been likely to create. I thought her more like him than ever I had thought her; and I felt, rather than saw, that the resemblance was not lost on my companion.*

She sat upright in her arm-chair, with a stately, immovable, passionless air, that it seemed as if nothing could disturb. She looked very steadfastly at Mr. Peggotty when he stood before her; and he looked quite as steadfastly at her. Rosa Dartle's keen glance comprehended all of us. For some moments not a word was spoken.

She motioned to Mr. Peggotty to be seated. He said, in a low voice, 'I shouldn't feel it nat'ral, ma'am, to sit down in this house. I'd sooner stand.' And this was succeeded by another silence, which she broke thus:

'I know, with deep regret, what has brought you here. What do you want of me? What do you ask me to do?'

He put his hat under his arm, and feeling in his breast for Emily's letter, took it out, unfolded it, and gave it to her. 'Please to read that, ma'am. That's my niece's hand!'

She read it, in the same stately and impassive way, — untouched by its contents, as far as I could see, — and returned it to him.

'"Unless he brings me back a lady,"' said Mr. Peggotty, tracing out that part with his finger. 'I come to know, ma'am, whether he will keep his wured?'

'No,' she returned.

'Why not?' said Mr. Peggotty.

'It is impossible. He would disgrace himself. You cannot fail to know that she is far below him.'

'Raise her up!' said Mr. Peggotty.

'She is uneducated and ignorant.'

'Maybe she's not; maybe she is,' said Mr. Peggotty. 'I think not, ma'am; but I'm no judge of them things. Teach her better!'

'Since you oblige me to speak more plainly, which I am very unwilling to do, her humble connexions would render such a thing impossible, if nothing else did.'

'Hark to this, ma'am,' he returned, slowly and quietly. 'You know what it is to love your child. So do I. If she was a hundred times my child, I couldn't love her more. You doen't know what it is to lose your child. I do. All the heaps of riches in the wureld would be nowt to me (if they was mine) to buy her back! But, save her from this disgrace, and she shall never be disgraced by us. Not one of us that she's growed up among, not one of us that's lived along with her and had her for their all in all, these many year, will ever look upon her pritty face again. We'll be content to let her be; we'll be content to think of her, far off, as if she was underneath another sun and sky; we'll be content to trust her to her husband, – to her little children, p'raps, – and bide the time when all of us shall be alike in quality afore our God!'

My Aunt Astonishes Me

From Chapter XXXIV: "My Aunt Astonishes Me"

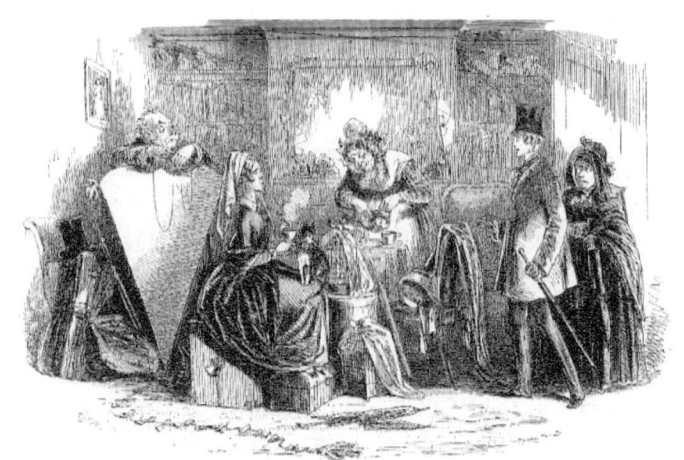

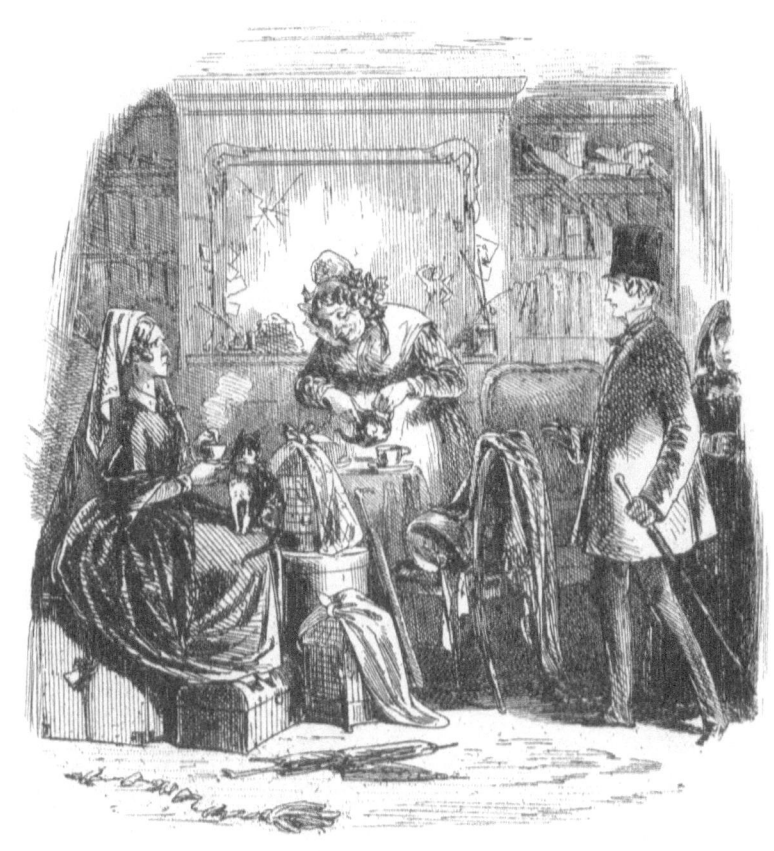

*W*e were both very much surprised, coming higher up, to find my outer door standing open (which I had shut) and to hear voices inside.

We looked at one another, without knowing what to make of this, and went into the sitting-room. What was my amazement to find, of all people upon earth, my aunt there, and Mr. Dick! My aunt sitting on a quantity of luggage, with her two birds before her, and her cat on her knee, like a female Robinson Crusoe, drinking tea. Mr. Dick leaning thoughtfully on a great kite, such as we had often been out together to fly, with more luggage piled about him!

'My dear aunt!' cried I. 'Why, what an unexpected pleasure!'

We cordially embraced; and Mr. Dick and I cordially shook hands; and Mrs. Crupp, who was busy making tea, and could not be too attentive, cordially said she had knowed well as Mr. Copperfull would have his heart in his mouth, when he see his dear relations.

'Holloa!' said my aunt to Peggotty, who quailed before her awful presence. 'How are YOU?'

'You remember my aunt, Peggotty?' said I.

'For the love of goodness, child,' exclaimed my aunt, 'don't call the woman by that South Sea Island name! If she married and got rid of it, which was the best thing she could do, why don't you give her the benefit of the change? What's your name now, − P?' said my aunt, as a compromise for the obnoxious appellation.

'Barkis, ma'am,' said Peggotty, with a curtsey.

'Well! That's human,' said my aunt. 'It sounds less as if you wanted a missionary. How d'ye do, Barkis? I hope you're well?'

Encouraged by these gracious words, and by my aunt's ex-

tending her hand, Barkis came forward, and took the hand, and curtseyed her acknowledgements.

'We are older than we were, I see,' said my aunt. 'We have only met each other once before, you know. A nice business we made of it then! Trot, my dear, another cup.'

Mr. Wickfield And His Partner Wait Upon My Aunt

From Chapter XXXV: "Depression"

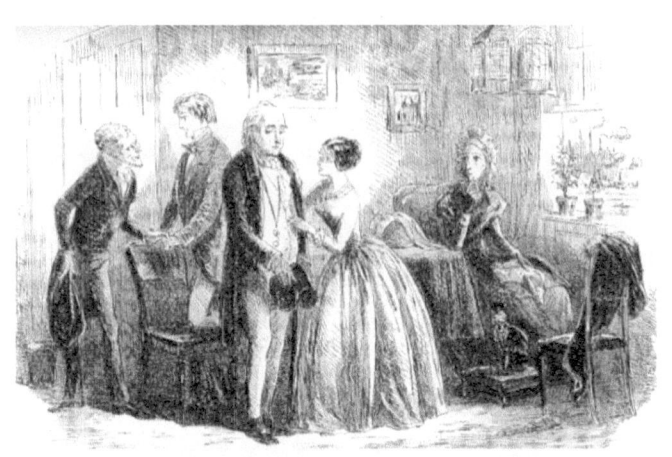

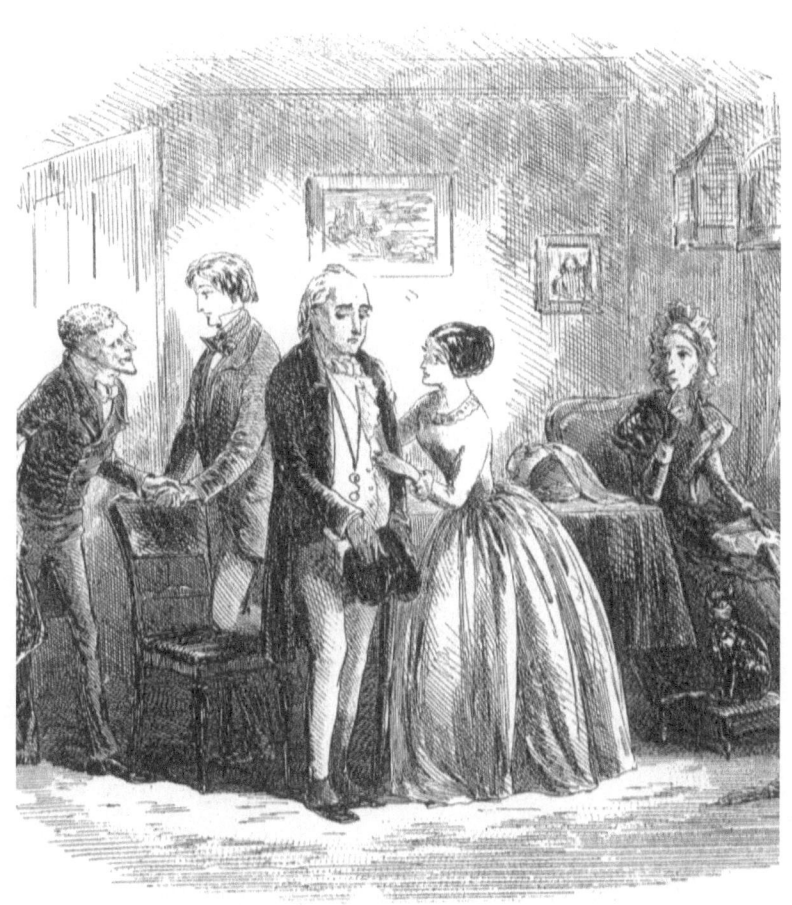

I opened the door, and admitted, not only Mr. Wickfield, but Uriah Heep. I had not seen Mr. Wickfield for some time. I was prepared for a great change in him, after what I had heard from Agnes, but his appearance shocked me.

It was not that he looked many years older, though still dressed with the old scrupulous cleanliness; or that there was an unwholesome ruddiness upon his face; or that his eyes were full and bloodshot; or that there was a nervous trembling in his hand, the cause of which I knew, and had for some years seen at work. It was not that he had lost his good looks, or his old bearing of a gentleman – for that he had not – but the thing that struck me most, was, that with the evidences of his native superiority still upon him, he should submit himself to that crawling impersonation of meanness, Uriah Heep. The reversal of the two natures, in their relative positions, Uriah's of power and Mr. Wickfield's of dependence, was a sight more painful to me than I can express. If I had seen an Ape taking command of a Man, I should hardly have thought it a more degrading spectacle.

He appeared to be only too conscious of it himself. When he came in, he stood still; and with his head bowed, as if he felt it. This was only for a moment; for Agnes softly said to him, 'Papa! Here is Miss Trotwood – and Trotwood, whom you have not seen for a long while!' and then he approached, and constrainedly gave my aunt his hand, and shook hands more cordially with me. In the moment's pause I speak of, I saw Uriah's countenance form itself into a most ill-favoured smile. Agnes saw it too, I think, for she shrank from him.

What my aunt saw, or did not see, I defy the science of physiognomy to have made out, without her own consent. I believe there never was anybody with such an imperturbable countenance when she chose. Her face might have been a dead-wall on the occasion in question, for any light it threw upon her thoughts; until she broke silence with her usual abruptness.

'Well, Wickfield!' said my aunt; and he looked up at her for the first time. 'I have been telling your daughter how well I have been disposing of my money for myself, because I couldn't trust it to you, as you were growing rusty in business matters. We have been taking counsel together, and getting on very well, all things considered. Agnes is worth the whole firm, in my opinion.'

'If I may umbly make the remark,' said Uriah Heep, with a writhe, 'I fully agree with Miss Betsey Trotwood, and should be only too appy if Miss Agnes was a partner.'

'You're a partner yourself, you know,' returned my aunt, 'and that's about enough for you, I expect. How do you find yourself, sir?'

In acknowledgement of this question, addressed to him with extraordinary curtness, Mr. Heep, uncomfortably clutching the blue bag he carried, replied that he was pretty well, he thanked my aunt, and hoped she was the same.

'And you, Master – I should say, Mister Copperfield,' pursued Uriah. 'I hope I see you well! I am rejoiced to see you, Mister Copperfield, even under present circumstances.' I believed that; for he seemed to relish them very much. 'Present circumstances is not what your friends would wish for you, Mister Copperfield, but it isn't money makes the man: it's – I am really unequal with my umble powers to express what it is,' said Uriah, with a fawning jerk, 'but it isn't money!'

Here he shook hands with me: not in the common way, but standing at a good distance from me, and lifting my hand up and down like a pump handle, that he was a little afraid of.

'And how do you think we are looking, Master Copperfield,

– I should say, Mister?' fawned Uriah. 'Don't you find Mr. Wickfield blooming, sir? Years don't tell much in our firm, Master Copperfield, except in raising up the umble, namely, mother and self – and in developing,' he added, as an after-thought, 'the beautiful, namely, Miss Agnes.'

He jerked himself about, after this compliment, in such an intolerable manner, that my aunt, who had sat looking straight at him, lost all patience.

'Deuce take the man!' said my aunt, sternly, 'what's he about? Don't be galvanic, sir!'

'I ask your pardon, Miss Trotwood,' returned Uriah; 'I'm aware you're nervous.'

'Go along with you, sir!' said my aunt, anything but ap-peased. 'Don't presume to say so! I am nothing of the sort. If you're an eel, sir, conduct yourself like one. If you're a man, con-trol your limbs, sir! Good God!' said my aunt, with great indig-nation, 'I am not going to be serpentined and corkscrewed out of my senses!'

Mr. Micawber Delivers Some Valedictory Remarks

From Chapter XXXVI: "Enthousiasm"

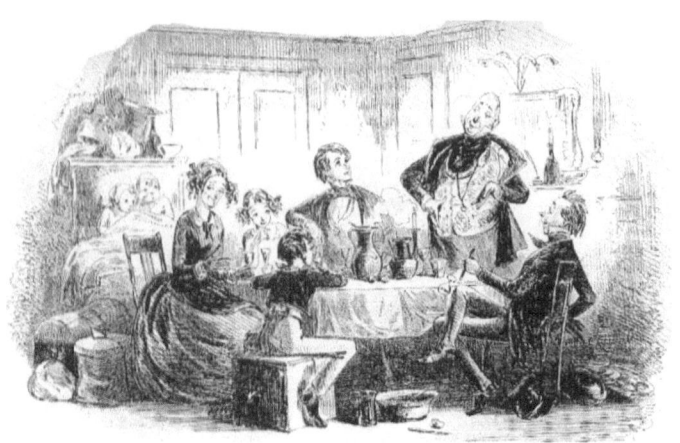

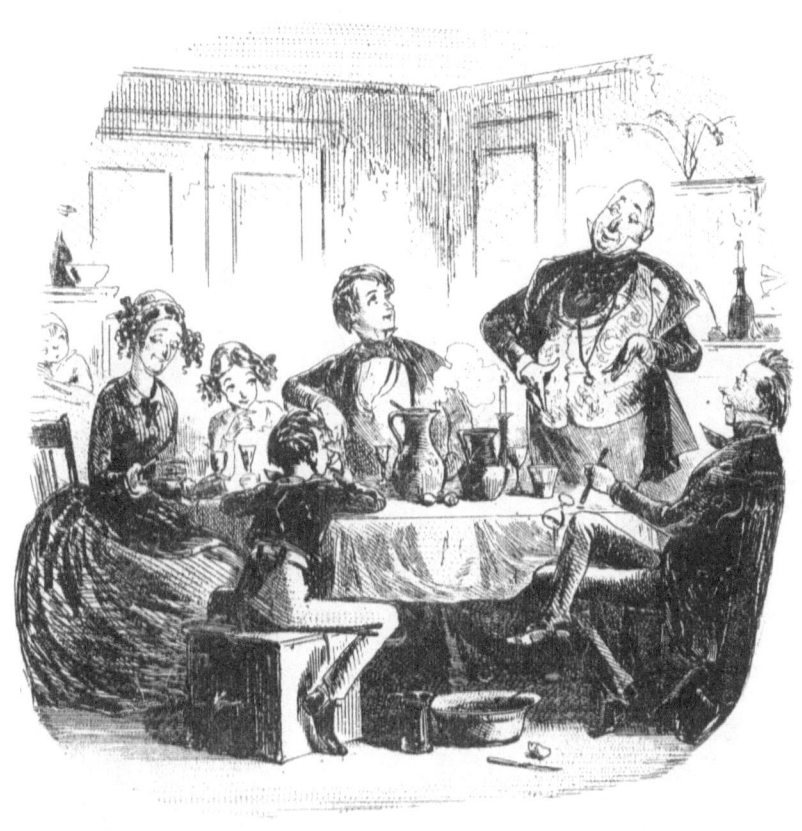

*M*y dear Copperfield,' said Mr. Micawber, rising with one of his thumbs in each of his waistcoat pockets, 'the companion of my youth: if I may be allowed the expression — and my esteemed friend Traddles: if I may be permitted to call him so — will allow me, on the part of Mrs. Micawber, myself, and our offspring, to thank them in the warmest and most uncompromising terms for their good wishes. It may be expected that on the eve of a migration which will consign us to a perfectly new existence,' Mr. Micawber spoke as if they were going five hundred thousand miles, 'I should offer a few valedictory remarks to two such friends as I see before me. But all that I have to say in this way, I have said. Whatever station in society I may attain, through the medium of the learned profession of which I am about to become an unworthy member, I shall endeavour not to disgrace, and Mrs. Micawber will be safe to adorn. Under the temporary pressure of pecuniary liabilities, contracted with a view to their immediate liquidation, but remaining unliquidated through a combination of circumstances, I have been under the necessity of assuming a garb from which my natural instincts recoil — I allude to spectacles — and possessing myself of a cognomen, to which I can establish no legitimate pretensions. All I have to say on that score is, that the cloud has passed from the dreary scene, and the God of Day is once more high upon the mountain tops. On Monday next, on the arrival of the four o'clock afternoon coach at Canterbury, my foot will be on my native heath — my name, Micawber!'

Traddles Makes A Figure In Parliament, And I Report Him

From Chapter XXXVIII: "A Dissolution Of Partnership"

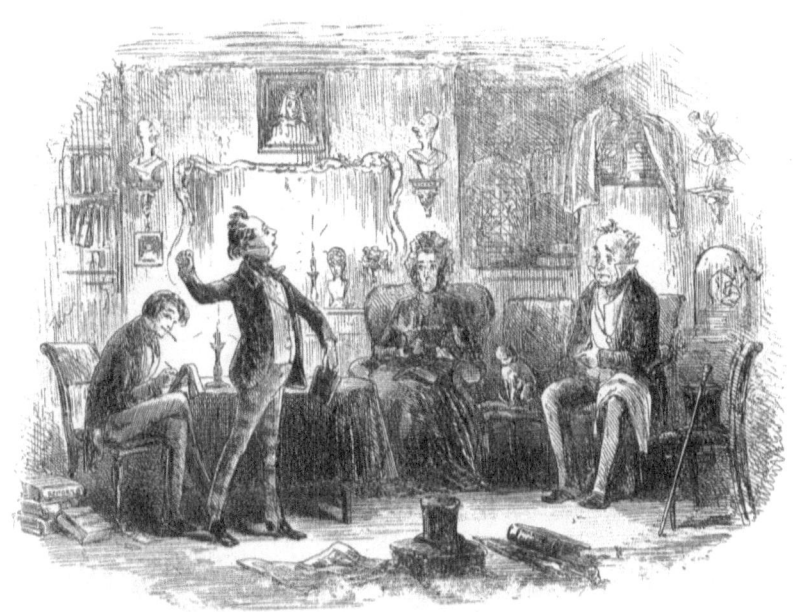

I should like to see such a Parliament anywhere else! My aunt and Mr. Dick represented the Government or the Opposition (as the case might be), and Traddles, with the assistance of Enfield's Speakers, or a volume of parliamentary orations, thundered astonishing invectives against them. Standing by the table, with his finger in the page to keep the place, and his right arm flourishing above his head, Traddles, as Mr. Pitt, Mr. Fox, Mr. Sheridan, Mr. Burke, Lord Castlereagh, Viscount Sidmouth, or Mr. Canning, would work himself into the most violent heats, and deliver the most withering denunciations of the profligacy and corruption of my aunt and Mr. Dick; while I used to sit, at a little distance, with my notebook on my knee, fagging after him with all my might and main. The inconsistency and recklessness of Traddles were not to be exceeded by any real politician. He was for any description of policy, in the compass of a week; and nailed all sorts of colours to every denomination of mast. My aunt, looking very like an immovable Chancellor of the Exchequer, would occasionally throw in an interruption or two, as 'Hear!' or 'No!' or 'Oh!' when the text seemed to require it: which was always a signal to Mr. Dick (a perfect country gentleman) to follow lustily with the same cry. But Mr. Dick got taxed with such things in the course of his Parliamentary career, and was made responsible for such awful consequences, that he became uncomfortable in his mind sometimes. I believe he actually began to be afraid he really had been doing something, tending to the annihilation of the British constitution, and the ruin of the country.

The Wanderer

From Chapter XL: "The Wanderer"

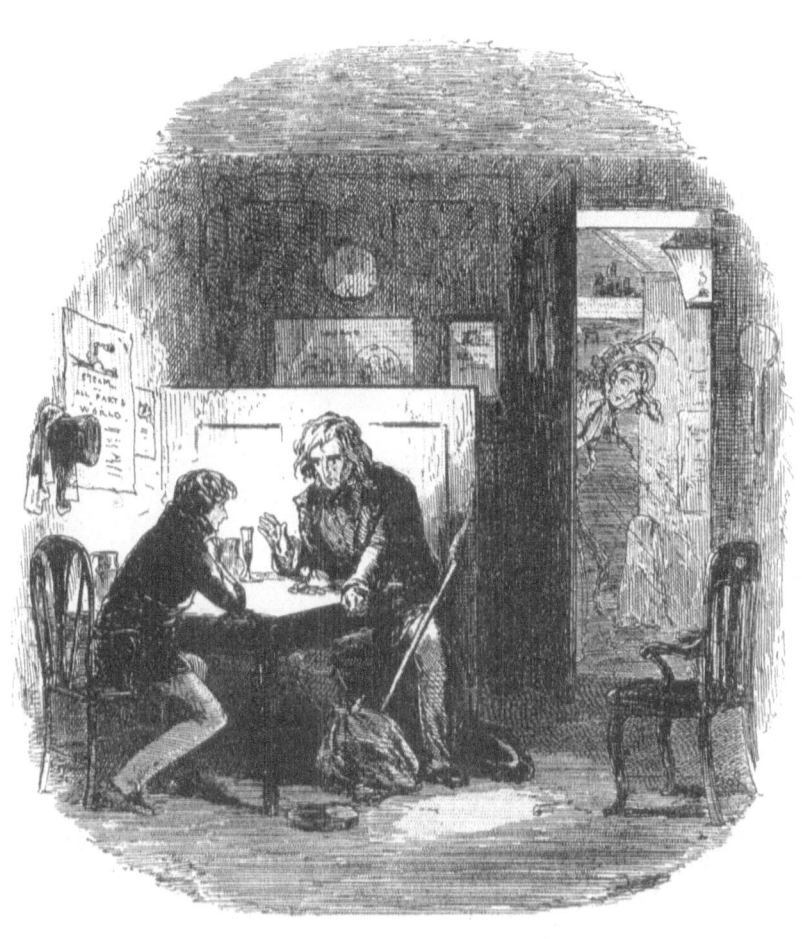

*I*n those days there was a side-entrance to the stable-yard of the Golden Cross, the inn so memorable to me in connexion with his misfortune, nearly opposite to where we stood. I pointed out the gateway, put my arm through his, and we went across. Two or three public-rooms opened out of the stable-yard; and looking into one of them, and finding it empty, and a good fire burning, I took him in there.

When I saw him in the light, I observed, not only that his hair was long and ragged, but that his face was burnt dark by the sun. He was greyer, the lines in his face and forehead were deeper, and he had every appearance of having toiled and wandered through all varieties of weather; but he looked very strong, and like a man upheld by steadfastness of purpose, whom nothing could tire out. He shook the snow from his hat and clothes, and brushed it away from his face, while I was inwardly making these remarks. As he sat down opposite to me at a table, with his back to the door by which we had entered, he put out his rough hand again, and grasped mine warmly.

'I'll tell you, Mas'r Davy,' he said, – 'wheer all I've been, and what-all we've heerd. I've been fur, and we've heerd little; but I'll tell you!'

I rang the bell for something hot to drink. He would have nothing stronger than ale; and while it was being brought, and being warmed at the fire, he sat thinking. There was a fine, massive gravity in his face, I did not venture to disturb.

'When she was a child,' he said, lifting up his head soon after we were left alone, 'she used to talk to me a deal about the sea, and about them coasts where the sea got to be dark blue, and to lay a-shining and a-shining in the sun. I thowt, odd times, as her father being drownded made her think on it so much. I doen't know, you see, but maybe she believed – or hoped

– he had drifted out to them parts, where the flowers is always a-blowing, and the country bright.'

'It is likely to have been a childish fancy,' I replied.

'When she was – lost,' said Mr. Peggotty, 'I know'd in my mind, as he would take her to them countries. I know'd in my mind, as he'd have told her wonders of 'em, and how she was to be a lady theer, and how he got her to listen to him fust, along o' sech like. When we see his mother, I know'd quite well as I was right. I went across-channel to France, and landed theer, as if I'd fell down from the sky.'

I saw the door move, and the snow drift in. I saw it move a little more, and a hand softly interpose to keep it open.

'I found out an English gen'leman as was in authority,' said Mr. Peggotty, 'and told him I was a-going to seek my niece. He got me them papers as I wanted fur to carry me through – I doen't rightly know how they're called – and he would have give me money, but that I was thankful to have no need on. I thank him kind, for all he done, I'm sure! "I've wrote afore you," he says to me, "and I shall speak to many as will come that way, and many will know you, fur distant from here, when you're a-travelling alone." I told him, best as I was able, what my grati-toode was, and went away through France.'

'Alone, and on foot?' said I.

'Mostly a-foot,' he rejoined; 'sometimes in carts along with people going to market; sometimes in empty coaches. Many mile a day a-foot, and often with some poor soldier or another, trav-elling to see his friends. I couldn't talk to him,' said Mr. Peggot-ty, 'nor he to me; but we was company for one another, too, along the dusty roads.'

I should have known that by his friendly tone.

'When I come to any town,' he pursued, 'I found the inn,

and waited about the yard till someone turned up (someone mostly did) as know'd English. Then I told how that I was on my way to seek my niece, and they told me what manner of gentlefolks was in the house, and I waited to see any as seemed like her, going in or out. When it warn't Em'ly, I went on agen. By little and little, when I come to a new village or that, among the poor people, I found they know'd about me. They would set me down at their cottage doors, and give me what-not fur to eat and drink, and show me where to sleep; and many a woman, Mas'r Davy, as has had a daughter of about Em'ly's age, I've found a-waiting fur me, at Our Saviour's Cross outside the village, fur to do me sim'lar kindnesses. Some has had daughters as was dead. And God only knows how good them mothers was to me!'

It was Martha at the door. I saw her haggard, listening face distinctly. My dread was lest he should turn his head, and see her too.

Traddles And I In Conference With The Misses Spenlow

From Chapter XLI: "Dora's Aunts"

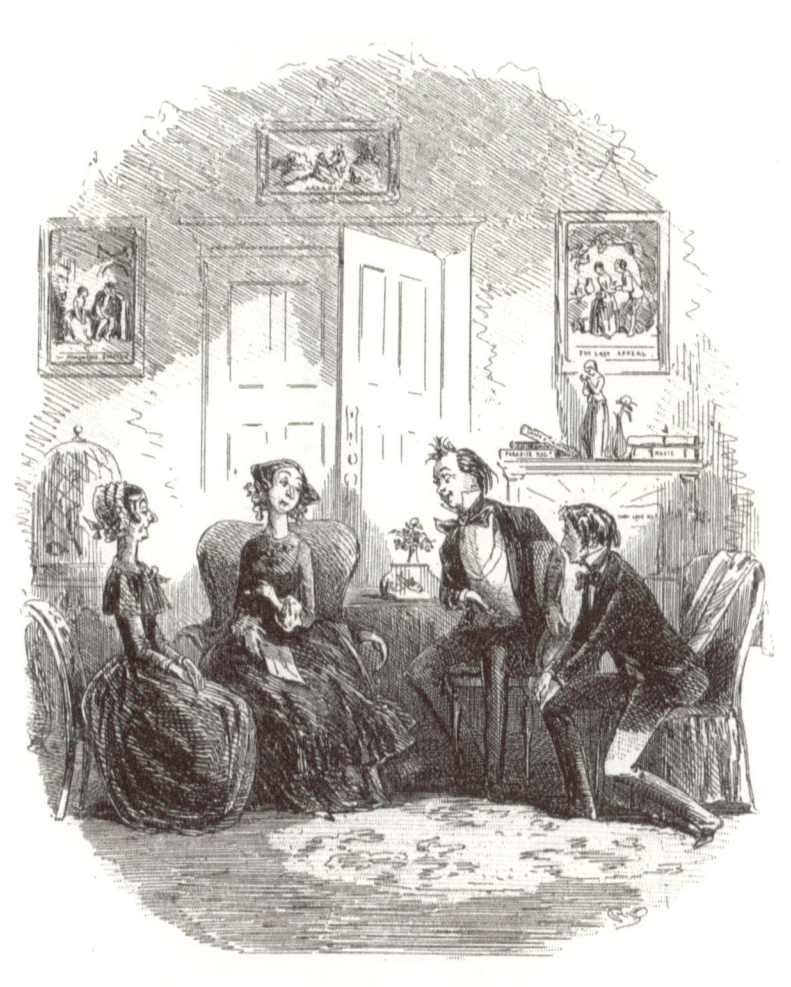

*W*hen I had done tumbling over Traddles, and had sat upon something which was not a cat — my first seat was — I so far recovered my sight, as to perceive that Mr. Spenlow had evidently been the youngest of the family; that there was a disparity of six or eight years between the two sisters; and that the younger appeared to be the manager of the conference, inasmuch as she had my letter in her hand — so familiar as it looked to me, and yet so odd! — and was referring to it through an eye-glass. They were dressed alike, but this sister wore her dress with a more youthful air than the other; and perhaps had a trifle more frill, or tucker, or brooch, or bracelet, or some little thing of that kind, which made her look more lively. They were both upright in their carriage, formal, precise, composed, and quiet. The sister who had not my letter, had her arms crossed on her breast, and resting on each other, like an Idol.

'Mr. Copperfield, I believe,' said the sister who had got my letter, addressing herself to Traddles.

This was a frightful beginning. Traddles had to indicate that I was Mr. Copperfield, and I had to lay claim to myself, and they had to divest themselves of a preconceived opinion that Traddles was Mr. Copperfield, and altogether we were in a nice condition. To improve it, we all distinctly heard Jip give two short barks, and receive another choke.

I Am Married

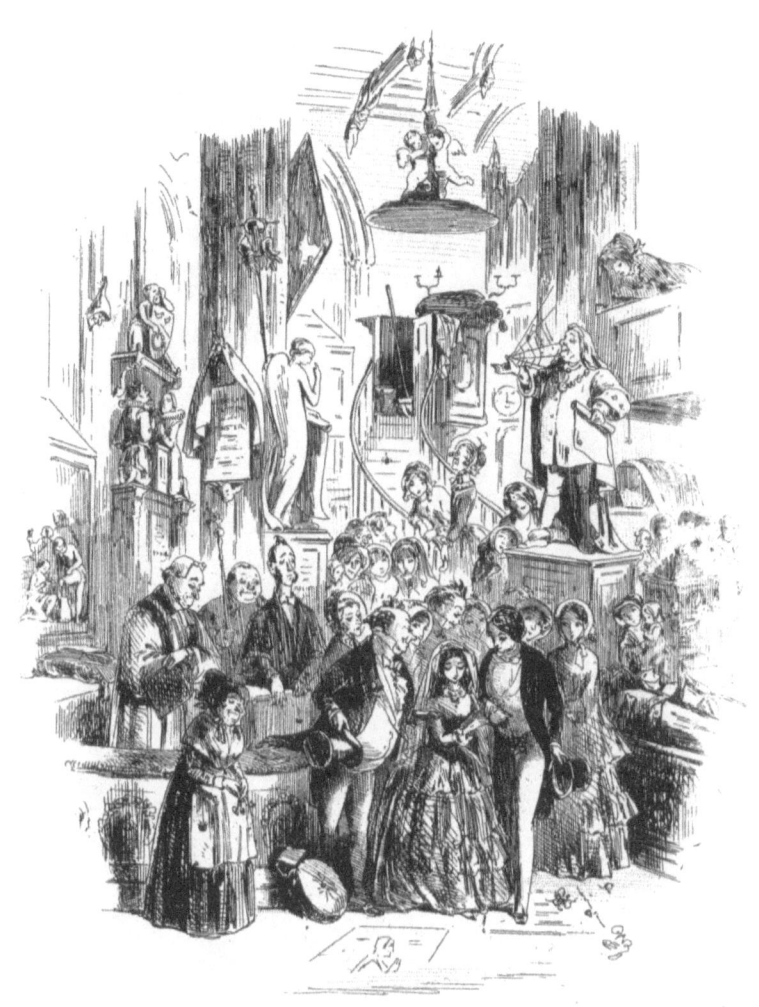

*M*y aunt sits with my hand in hers all the way. When we stop a little way short of the church, to put down Peggotty, whom we have brought on the box, she gives it a squeeze, and me a kiss.

'God bless you, Trot! My own boy never could be dearer. I think of poor dear Baby this morning.' 'So do I. And of all I owe to you, dear aunt.'

'Tut, child!' says my aunt; and gives her hand in overflowing cordiality to Traddles, who then gives his to Mr. Dick, who then gives his to me, who then gives mine to Traddles, and then we come to the church door.

The church is calm enough, I am sure; but it might be a steam-power loom in full action, for any sedative effect it has on me. I am too far gone for that.

The rest is all a more or less incoherent dream.

A dream of their coming in with Dora; of the pew-opener arranging us, like a drill-sergeant, before the altar rails; of my wondering, even then, why pew-openers must always be the most disagreeable females procurable, and whether there is any religious dread of a disastrous infection of good-humour which renders it indispensable to set those vessels of vinegar upon the road to Heaven.

Of the clergyman and clerk appearing; of a few boatmen and some other people strolling in; of an ancient mariner behind me, strongly flavouring the church with rum; of the service beginning in a deep voice, and our all being very attentive.

Of Miss Lavinia, who acts as a semi-auxiliary bridesmaid, being the first to cry, and of her doing homage (as I take it) to the memory of Pidger, in sobs; of Miss Clarissa applying a smelling-bottle; of Agnes taking care of Dora; of my aunt endeavouring to represent herself as a model of sternness, with tears rolling down her face; of little Dora trembling very much, and making her responses in faint whispers.

Of our kneeling down together, side by side; of Dora's trembling less and less, but always clasping Agnes by the hand; of the service being got through, quietly and gravely; of our all looking at each other in an April state of smiles and tears, when it is over; of my young wife being hysterical in the vestry, and crying for her poor papa, her dear papa.

Of her soon cheering up again, and our signing the register all round. Of my going into the gallery for Peggotty to bring her to sign it; of Peggotty's hugging me in a corner, and telling me she saw my own dear mother married; of its being over, and our going away.

Of my walking so proudly and lovingly down the aisle with my sweet wife upon my arm, through a mist of half-seen people, pulpits, monuments, pews, fonts, organs, and church windows, in which there flutter faint airs of association with my childish church at home, so long ago.

Of their whispering, as we pass, what a youthful couple we are, and what a pretty little wife she is. Of our all being so merry and talkative in the carriage going back. Of Sophy telling us that when she saw Traddles (whom I had entrusted with the licence) asked for it, she almost fainted, having been convinced that he would contrive to lose it, or to have his pocket picked. Of Agnes laughing gaily; and of Dora being so fond of Agnes that she will not be separated from her, but still keeps her hand.

Our Housekeeping

From Chapter XLIV: "Our Housekeeping"

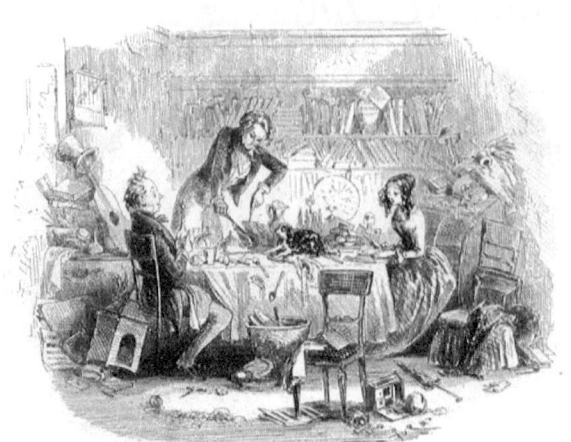

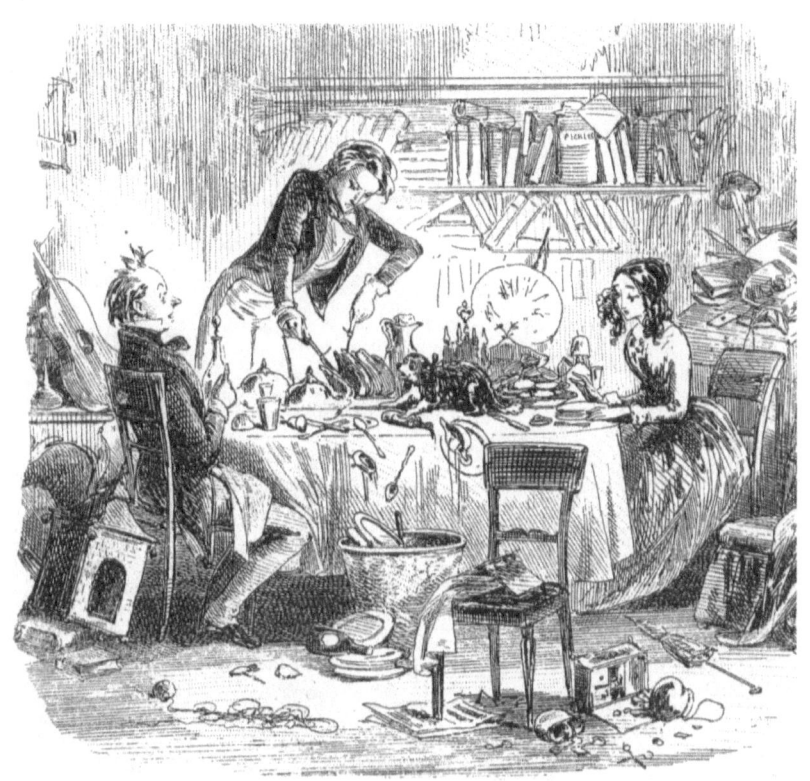

One of our first feats in the housekeeping way was a little dinner to Traddles. I met him in town, and asked him to walk out with me that afternoon. He readily consenting, I wrote to Dora, saying I would bring him home. It was pleasant weather, and on the road we made my domestic happiness the theme of conversation. Traddles was very full of it; and said, that, picturing himself with such a home, and Sophy waiting and preparing for him, he could think of nothing wanting to complete his bliss.

I could not have wished for a prettier little wife at the opposite end of the table, but I certainly could have wished, when we sat down, for a little more room. I did not know how it was, but though there were only two of us, we were at once always cramped for room, and yet had always room enough to lose everything in. I suspect it may have been because nothing had a place of its own, except Jip's pagoda, which invariably blocked up the main thoroughfare. On the present occasion, Traddles was so hemmed in by the pagoda and the guitar-case, and Dora's flower-painting, and my writing-table, that I had serious doubts of the possibility of his using his knife and fork; but he protested, with his own good-humour, 'Oceans of room, Copperfield! I assure you, Oceans!'

There was another thing I could have wished, namely, that Jip had never been encouraged to walk about the tablecloth during dinner. I began to think there was something disorderly in his being there at all, even if he had not been in the habit of putting his foot in the salt or the melted butter. On this occasion he seemed to think he was introduced expressly to keep Traddles at bay; and he barked at my old friend, and made short runs at his plate, with such undaunted pertinacity, that he may be said to have engrossed the conversation.

However, as I knew how tender-hearted my dear Dora was, and how sensitive she would be to any slight upon her favourite, I hinted no objection. For similar reasons I made no allusion to the skirmishing plates upon the floor; or to the disreputable appearance of the castors, which were all at sixes and sevens, and looked drunk; or to the further blockade of Traddles by wandering vegetable dishes and jugs. I could not help wondering in my own mind, as I contemplated the boiled leg of mutton before me, previous to carving it, how it came to pass that our joints of meat were of such extraordinary shapes — and whether our butcher contracted for all the deformed sheep that came into the world; but I kept my reflections to myself.

'My love,' said I to Dora, 'what have you got in that dish?'

I could not imagine why Dora had been making tempting little faces at me, as if she wanted to kiss me.

'Oysters, dear,' said Dora, timidly.

'Was that YOUR thought?' said I, delighted.

'Ye-yes, Doady,' said Dora.

'There never was a happier one!' I exclaimed, laying down the carving-knife and fork. 'There is nothing Traddles likes so much!'

'Ye-yes, Doady,' said Dora, 'and so I bought a beautiful little barrel of them, and the man said they were very good. But I — I am afraid there's something the matter with them. They don't seem right.' Here Dora shook her head, and diamonds twinkled in her eyes.

'They are only opened in both shells,' said I. 'Take the top one off, my love.'

'But it won't come off!' said Dora, trying very hard, and looking very much distressed.

'Do you know, Copperfield,' said Traddles, cheerfully examining the dish, 'I think it is in consequence — they are capital oysters, but I think it is in consequence — of their never having been opened.'

They never had been opened; and we had no oyster-knives — and couldn't have used them if we had; so we looked at the oysters and ate the mutton. At least we ate as much of it as was done, and made up with capers. If I had permitted him, I am satisfied that Traddles would have made a perfect savage of himself, and eaten a plateful of raw meat, to express enjoyment of the repast; but I would hear of no such immolation on the altar of friendship, and we had a course of bacon instead; there happening, by good fortune, to be cold bacon in the larder.

Mr. Dick Fulfils My Aunt's Prediction

From Chapter XLV: "Mr. Dick Fulfils My Aunt's Prediction"

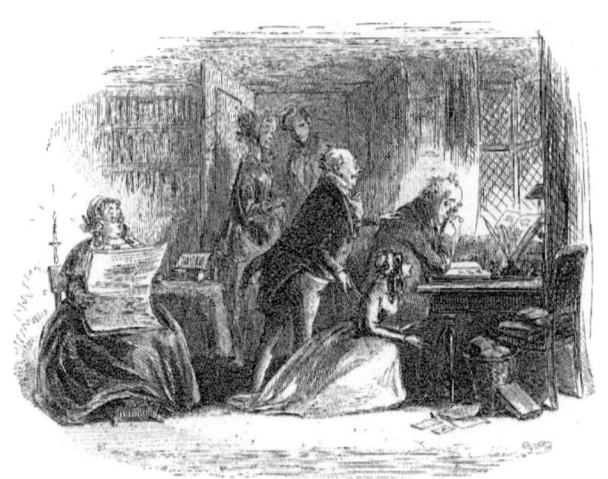

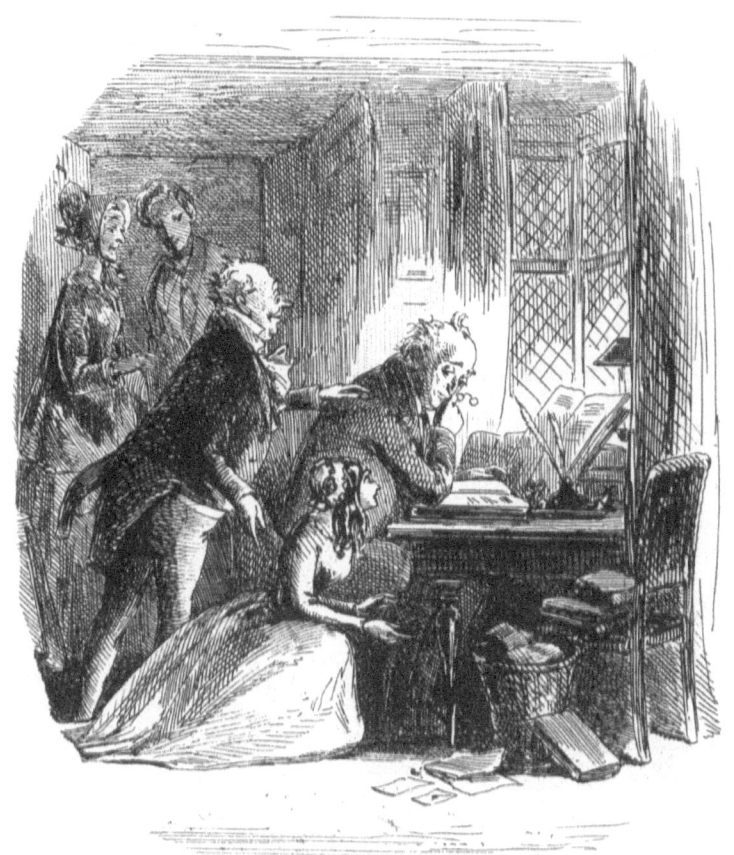

I was conscious of Mr. Dick's standing in the shadow of the room, shutting up his knife, when we accompanied her to the Study; and of my aunt's rubbing her nose violently, by the way, as a mild vent for her intolerance of our military friend; but who got first into the Study, or how Mrs. Markleham settled herself in a moment in her easy-chair, or how my aunt and I came to be left together near the door (unless her eyes were quicker than mine, and she held me back), I have forgotten, if I ever knew. But this I know, — that we saw the Doctor before he saw us, sitting at his table, among the folio volumes in which he delighted, resting his head calmly on his hand. That, in the same moment, we saw Mrs. Strong glide in, pale and trembling. That Mr. Dick supported her on his arm. That he laid his other hand upon the Doctor's arm, causing him to look up with an abstracted air. That, as the Doctor moved his head, his wife dropped down on one knee at his feet, and, with her hands imploringly lifted, fixed upon his face the memorable look I had never forgotten. That at this sight Mrs. Markleham dropped the newspaper, and stared more like a figure-head intended for a ship to be called The Astonishment, than anything else I can think of.

The gentleness of the Doctor's manner and surprise, the dignity that mingled with the supplicating attitude of his wife, the amiable concern of Mr. Dick, and the earnestness with which my aunt said to herself, 'That man mad!' (triumphantly expressive of the misery from which she had saved him) — I see and hear, rather than remember, as I write about it.

'Doctor!' said Mr. Dick. 'What is it that's amiss? Look here!'

'Annie!' cried the Doctor. 'Not at my feet, my dear!'

'Yes!' she said. 'I beg and pray that no one will leave the room! Oh, my husband and father, break this long silence. Let us both know what it is that has come between us!'

Mrs. Markleham, by this time recovering the power of speech, and seeming to swell with family pride and motherly indignation, here exclaimed, 'Annie, get up immediately, and don't disgrace everybody belonging to you by humbling yourself like that, unless you wish to see me go out of my mind on the spot!'

'Mama!' returned Annie. 'Waste no words on me, for my appeal is to my husband, and even you are nothing here.'

'Nothing!' exclaimed Mrs. Markleham. 'Me, nothing! The child has taken leave of her senses. Please to get me a glass of water!'

I was too attentive to the Doctor and his wife, to give any heed to this request; and it made no impression on anybody else; so Mrs. Markleham panted, stared, and fanned herself.

'Annie!' said the Doctor, tenderly taking her in his hands. 'My dear! If any unavoidable change has come, in the sequence of time, upon our married life, you are not to blame. The fault is mine, and only mine. There is no change in my affection, admiration, and respect. I wish to make you happy. I truly love and honour you. Rise, Annie, pray!'

But she did not rise. After looking at him for a little while, she sank down closer to him, laid her arm across his knee, and dropping her head upon it, said:

'If I have any friend here, who can speak one word for me, or for my husband in this matter; if I have any friend here, who can give a voice to any suspicion that my heart has sometimes whispered to me; if I have any friend here, who honours my husband, or has ever cared for me, and has anything within his knowledge, no matter what it is, that may help to mediate between us, I implore that friend to speak!'

There was a profound silence. After a few moments of pain-ful hesitation, I broke the silence.

The River

From Chapter XLVII: "Martha"

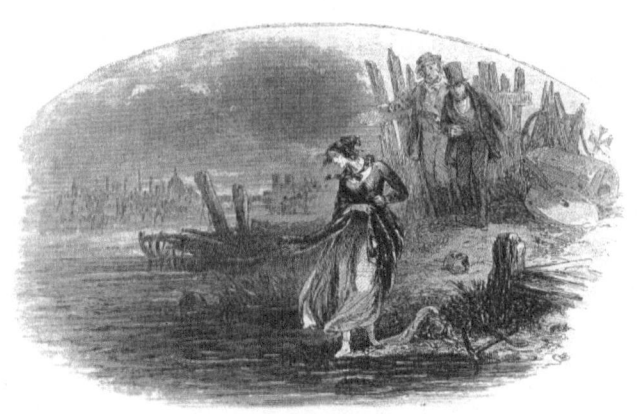

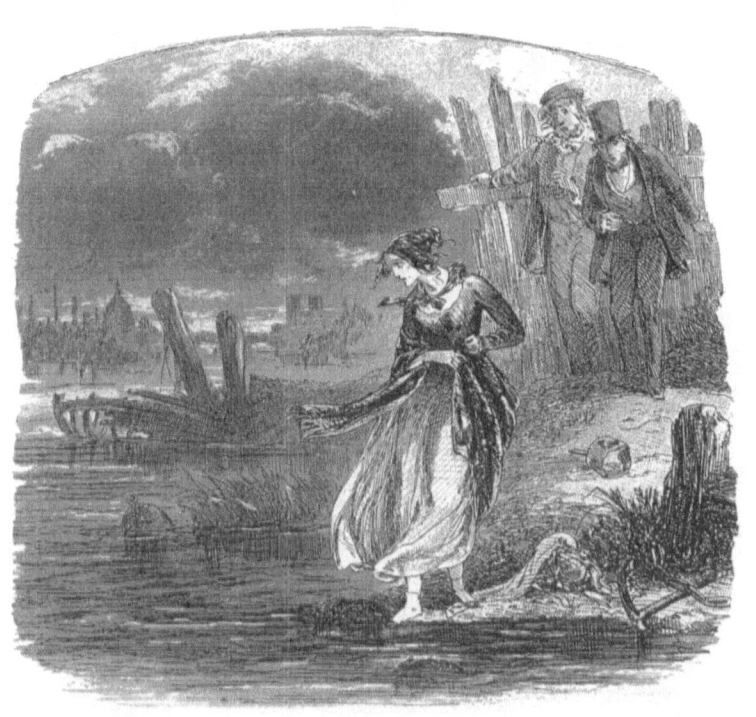

There was, and is when I write, at the end of that low-lying street, a dilapidated little wooden building, probably an obsolete old ferry-house. Its position is just at that point where the street ceases, and the road begins to lie between a row of houses and the river. As soon as she came here, and saw the water, she stopped as if she had come to her destination; and presently went slowly along by the brink of the river, looking intently at it.

All the way here, I had supposed that she was going to some house; indeed, I had vaguely entertained the hope that the house might be in some way associated with the lost girl. But that one dark glimpse of the river, through the gateway, had instinctively prepared me for her going no farther.

The neighbourhood was a dreary one at that time; as oppressive, sad, and solitary by night, as any about London. There were neither wharves nor houses on the melancholy waste of road near the great blank Prison. A sluggish ditch deposited its mud at the prison walls. Coarse grass and rank weeds straggled over all the marshy land in the vicinity. In one part, carcases of houses, inauspiciously begun and never finished, rotted away. In another, the ground was cumbered with rusty iron monsters of steam-boilers, wheels, cranks, pipes, furnaces, paddles, anchors, diving-bells, windmill-sails, and I know not what strange objects, accumulated by some speculator, and grovelling in the dust, underneath which — having sunk into the soil of their own weight in wet weather — they had the appearance of vainly trying to hide themselves. The clash and glare of sundry fiery Works upon the river-side, arose by night to disturb everything except the heavy and unbroken smoke that poured out of their chimneys. Slimy gaps and causeways, winding among old wooden piles, with a sickly substance clinging to the latter, like green hair, and the rags of last year's handbills offering rewards for drowned men fluttering above high-water mark, led down through the ooze and slush to the ebb-tide. There was a story that one of the pits dug for the dead in the time of the Great Plague was hereabout; and a blighting influence seemed to have proceeded from it over the whole place. Or else it looked as if it had gradually decomposed into that nightmare condition, out of the overflowings of the polluted stream.

As if she were a part of the refuse it had cast out, and left to corruption and decay, the girl we had followed strayed down to the river's brink, and stood in the midst of this night-picture, lonely and still, looking at the water.

There were some boats and barges astrand in the mud, and these enabled us to come within a few yards of her without being seen. I then signed to Mr. Peggotty to remain where he was, and emerged from their shade to speak to her. I did not approach her solitary figure without trembling; for this gloomy end to her determined walk, and the way in which she stood, almost within the cavernous shadow of the iron bridge, looking at the lights crookedly reflected in the strong tide, inspired a dread within me.

I think she was talking to herself. I am sure, although absorbed in gazing at the water, that her shawl was off her shoulders, and that she was muffling her hands in it, in an unsettled and bewildered way, more like the action of a sleep-walker than a waking person. I know, and never can forget, that there was that in her wild manner which gave me no assurance but that she would sink before my eyes, until I had her arm within my grasp.

At the same moment I said 'Martha!'

She uttered a terrified scream, and struggled with me with such strength that I doubt if I could have held her alone. But a stronger hand than mine was laid upon her; and when she raised her frightened eyes and saw whose it was, she made but one more effort and dropped down between us. We carried her away from the water to where there were some dry stones, and there laid her down, crying and moaning. In a little while she sat among the stones, holding her wretched head with both her hands.

'Oh, the river!' she cried passionately. 'Oh, the river!'

'Hush, hush!' said I. 'Calm yourself.'

But she still repeated the same words, continually exclaiming, 'Oh, the river!' over and over again.

'I know it's like me!' she exclaimed. 'I know that I belong to it. I know that it's the natural company of such as I am! It comes from country places, where there was once no harm in it – and it creeps through the dismal streets, defiled and miserable – and it goes away, like my life, to a great sea, that is always troubled – and I feel that I must go with it!' I have never known what despair was, except in the tone of those words.

'I can't keep away from it. I can't forget it. It haunts me day and night. It's the only thing in all the world that I am fit for, or that's fit for me. Oh, the dreadful river!'

Mr. Peggotty's Dream Comes True

From Chapter L: "Mr. Peggotty's Dream Comes True"

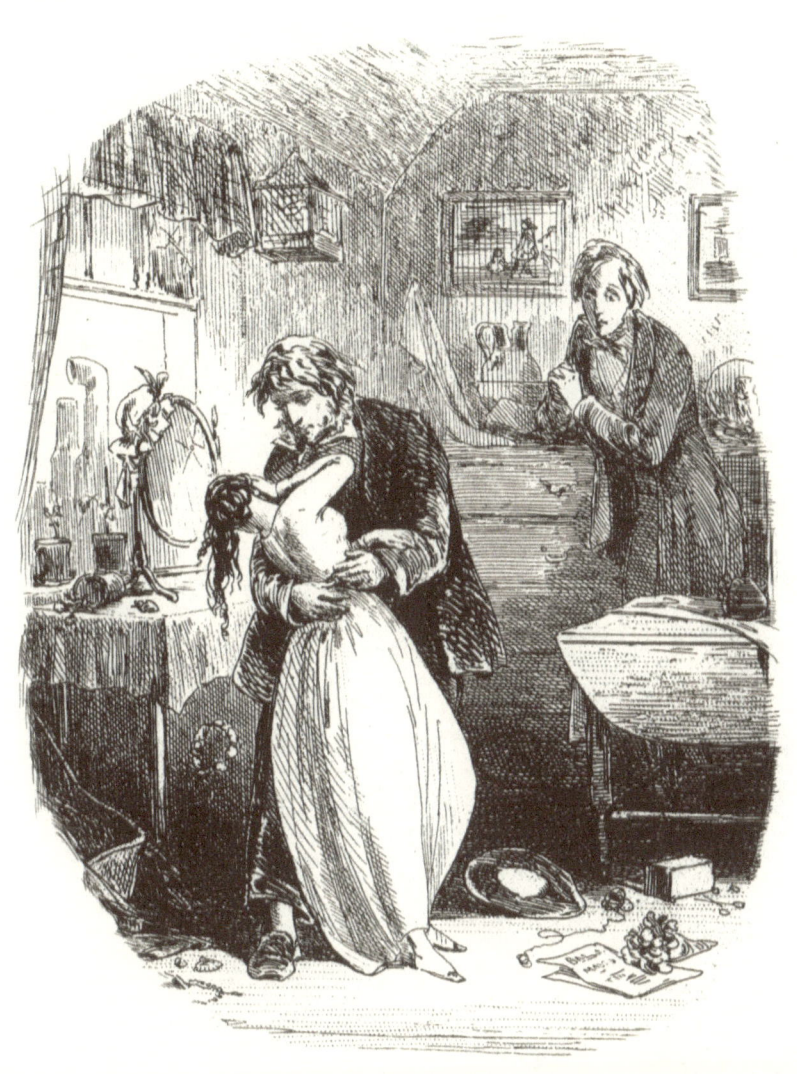

7 he foot upon the stairs came nearer – nearer – passed her as she went down – rushed into the room!

'Uncle!'

A fearful cry followed the word. I paused a moment, and looking in, saw him supporting her insensible figure in his arms. He gazed for a few seconds in the face; then stooped to kiss it – oh, how tenderly! – and drew a handkerchief before it.

'Mas'r Davy,' he said, in a low tremulous voice, when it was covered, 'I thank my Heav'nly Father as my dream's come true! I thank Him hearty for having guided of me, in His own ways, to my darling!'

With those words he took her up in his arms; and, with the veiled face lying on his bosom, and addressed towards his own, carried her, motionless and unconscious, down the stairs.

Restoration Of Mutual Confidence Between Mr. And Mrs. Micawber

From Chapter LII: "I Assist At An Explosion"

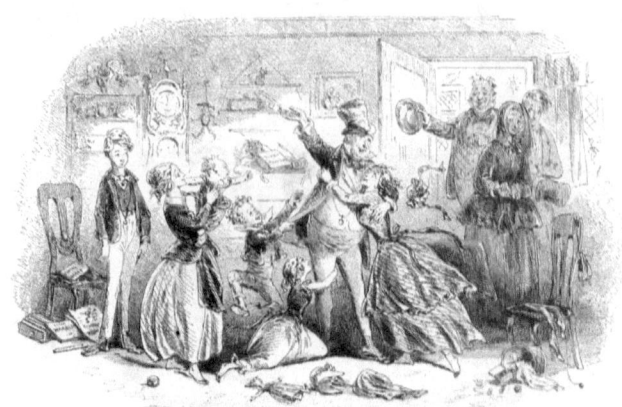

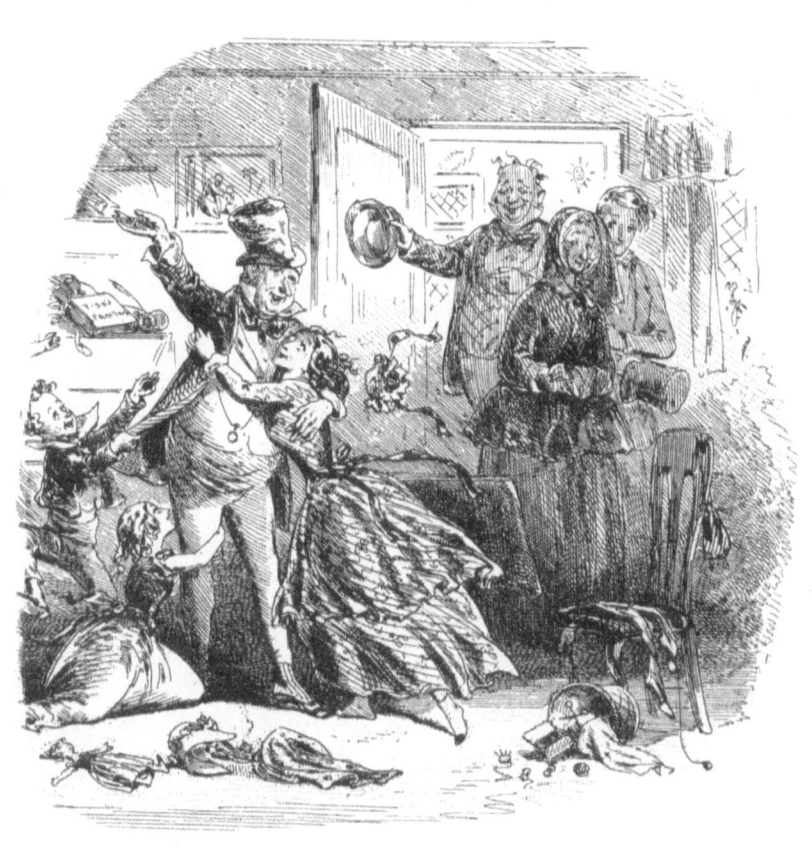

*H*is house was not far off; and as the street door opened into the sitting-room, and he bolted in with a precipitation quite his own, we found ourselves at once in the bosom of the family. Mr. Micawber exclaiming, 'Emma! my life!' rushed into Mrs. Micawber's arms. Mrs. Micawber shrieked, and folded Mr. Micawber in her embrace. Miss Micawber, nursing the unconscious stranger of Mrs. Micawber's last letter to me, was sensibly affected. The stranger leaped. The twins testified their joy by several inconvenient but innocent demonstrations. Master Micawber, whose disposition appeared to have been soured by early disappointment, and whose aspect had become morose, yielded to his better feelings, and blubbered.

'Emma!' said Mr. Micawber. 'The cloud is past from my mind. Mutual confidence, so long preserved between us once, is restored, to know no further interruption. Now, welcome poverty!' cried Mr. Micawber, shedding tears. 'Welcome misery, welcome houselessness, welcome hunger, rags, tempest, and beggary! Mutual confidence will sustain us to the end!'

With these expressions, Mr. Micawber placed Mrs. Micawber in a chair, and embraced the family all round; welcoming a variety of bleak prospects, which appeared, to the best of my judgement, to be anything but welcome to them; and calling upon them to come out into Canterbury and sing a chorus, as nothing else was left for their support.

My Child-Wife's Old Companion

From Chapter LIII: "Another Retrospect"

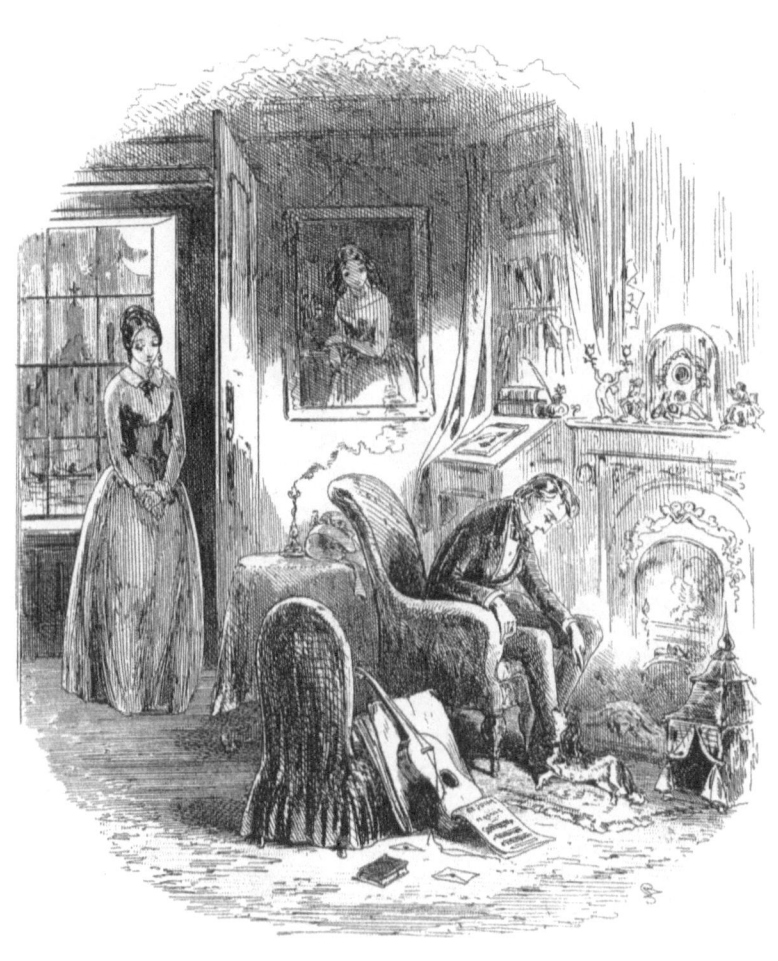

said that it was better as it is!' she whispers, as she holds me in her arms. 'Oh, Doady, after more years, you never could have loved your child-wife better than you do; and, after more years, she would so have tried and disappointed you, that you might not have been able to love her half so well! I know I was too young and foolish. It is much better as it is!'

Agnes is downstairs, when I go into the parlour; and I give her the message. She disappears, leaving me alone with Jip.

His Chinese house is by the fire; and he lies within it, on his bed of flannel, querulously trying to sleep. The bright moon is high and clear. As I look out on the night, my tears fall fast, and my undisciplined heart is chastened heavily – heavily.

I sit down by the fire, thinking with a blind remorse of all those secret feelings I have nourished since my marriage. I think of every little trifle between me and Dora, and feel the truth, that trifles make the sum of life. Ever rising from the sea of my remembrance, is the image of the dear child as I knew her first, graced by my young love, and by her own, with every fascination wherein such love is rich. Would it, indeed, have been better if we had loved each other as a boy and a girl, and forgotten it? Undisciplined heart, reply!

How the time wears, I know not; until I am recalled by my child-wife's old companion. More restless than he was, he crawls out of his house, and looks at me, and wanders to the door, and whines to go upstairs.

'Not tonight, Jip! Not tonight!'

He comes very slowly back to me, licks my hand, and lifts his dim eyes to my face.

'Oh, Jip! It may be, never again!'

He lies down at my feet, stretches himself out as if to sleep, and with a plaintive cry, is dead.

'Oh, Agnes! Look, look, here!'

- That face, so full of pity, and of grief, that rain of tears, that awful mute appeal to me, that solemn hand upraised towards Heaven!

'Agnes?'

It is over. Darkness comes before my eyes; and, for a time, all things are blotted out of my remembrance.

I Am The Bearer Of Evil Tidings

From Chapter LVI: "The New Wound, And The Old"

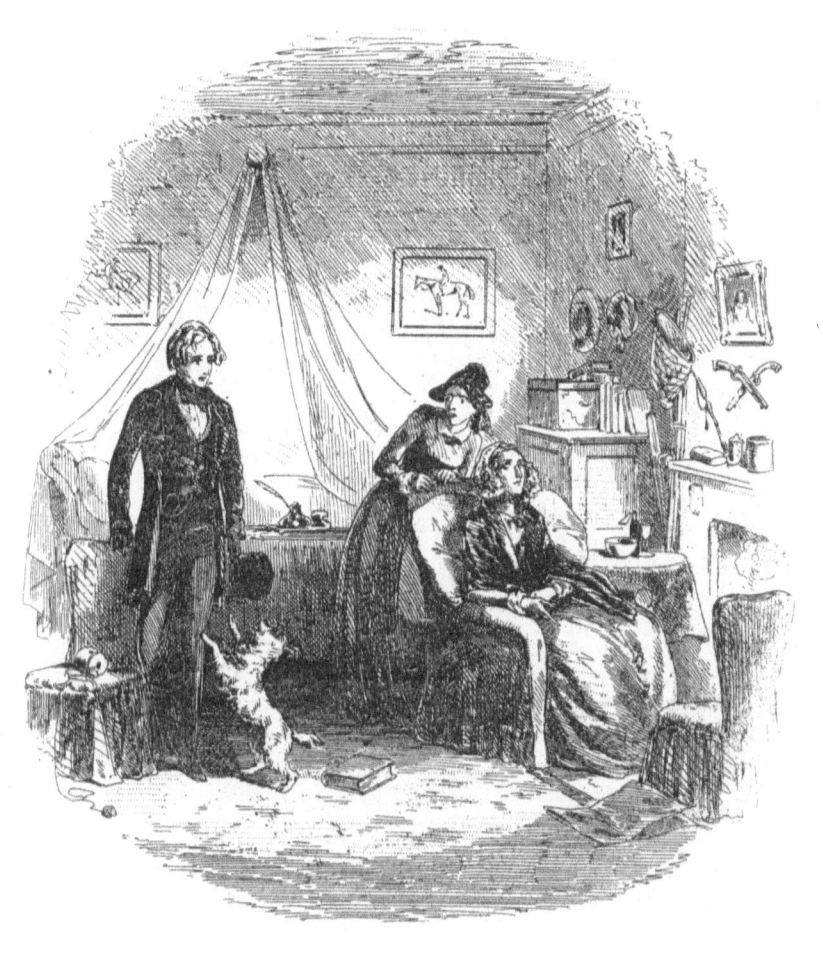

*A*t her chair, as usual, was Rosa Dartle. From the first moment of her dark eyes resting on me, I saw she knew I was the bearer of evil tidings. The scar sprung into view that instant. She withdrew herself a step behind the chair, to keep her own face out of Mrs. Steerforth's observation; and scrutinized me with a piercing gaze that never faltered, never shrunk.

'I am sorry to observe you are in mourning, sir,' said Mrs. Steerforth.

'I am unhappily a widower,' said I.

'You are very young to know so great a loss,' she returned. 'I am grieved to hear it. I am grieved to hear it. I hope Time will be good to you.'

'I hope Time,' said I, looking at her, 'will be good to all of us. Dear Mrs. Steerforth, we must all trust to that, in our heaviest misfortunes.'

The earnestness of my manner, and the tears in my eyes, alarmed her. The whole course of her thoughts appeared to stop, and change.

I tried to command my voice in gently saying his name, but it trembled. She repeated it to herself, two or three times, in a low tone. Then, addressing me, she said, with enforced calmness:

'My son is ill.'

'Very ill.'

'You have seen him?'

'I have.'

'Are you reconciled?'

I could not say Yes, I could not say No. She slightly turned her head towards the spot where Rosa Dartle had been standing at her elbow, and in that moment I said, by the motion of my lips, to Rosa, 'Dead!'

That Mrs. Steerforth might not be induced to look behind her, and read, plainly written, what she was not yet prepared to know, I met her look quickly; but I had seen Rosa Dartle throw her hands up in the air with vehemence of despair and horror, and then clasp them on her face.

The handsome lady – so like, oh so like! – regarded me with a fixed look, and put her hand to her forehead. I besought her to be calm, and prepare herself to bear what I had to tell; but I should rather have entreated her to weep, for she sat like a stone figure.

The Emigrants

From Chapter LVII: "The Emigrants"

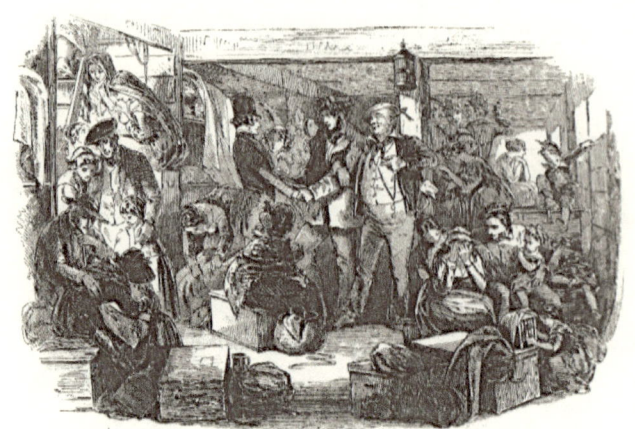

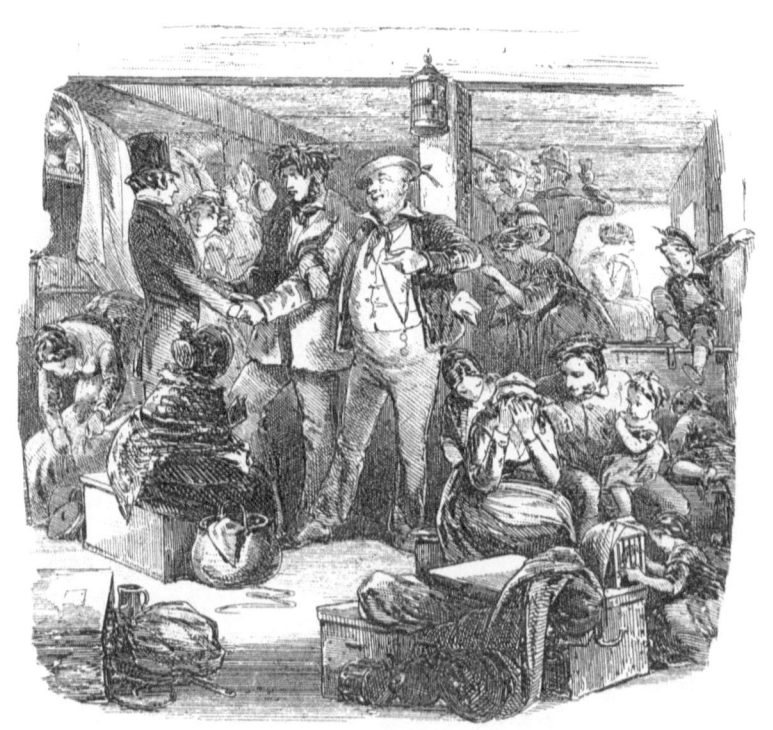

*M*r. Peggotty put down the two children he had been nursing, one on each knee, to join Mr. and Mrs. Micawber in drinking to all of us in return; and when he and the Micawbers cordially shook hands as comrades, and his brown face brightened with a smile, I felt that he would make his way, establish a good name, and be beloved, go where he would.

Even the children were instructed, each to dip a wooden spoon into Mr. Micawber's pot, and pledge us in its contents. When this was done, my aunt and Agnes rose, and parted from the emigrants. It was a sorrowful farewell. They were all crying; the children hung about Agnes to the last; and we left poor Mrs. Micawber in a very distressed condition, sobbing and weeping by a dim candle, that must have made the room look, from the river, like a miserable light-house.

I Am Shown Two Interesting Penitents

From Chapter LXI: "I Am Shown Two Interesting Penitents"

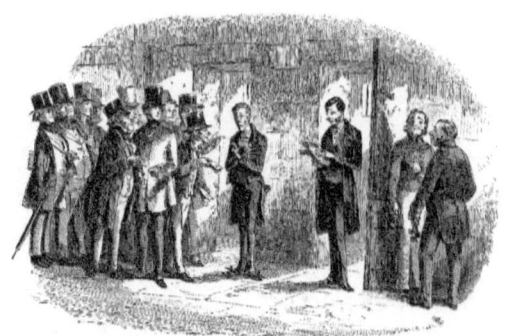

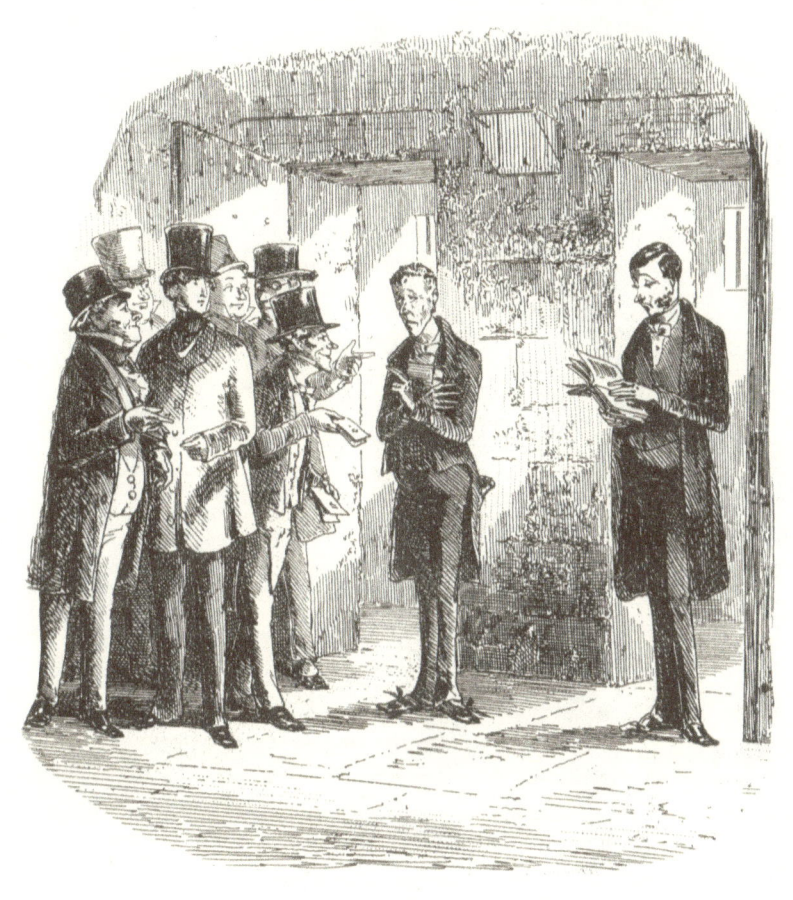

*H*owever, I heard so repeatedly, in the course of our goings to and fro, of a certain Number Twenty Seven, who was the Favourite, and who really appeared to be a Model Prisoner, that I resolved to suspend my judgement until I should see Twenty Seven. Twenty Eight, I understood, was also a bright particular star; but it was his misfortune to have his glory a little dimmed by the extraordinary lustre of Twenty Seven. I heard so much of Twenty Seven, of his pious admonitions to everybody around him, and of the beautiful letters he constantly wrote to his mother (whom he seemed to consider in a very bad way), that I became quite impatient to see him.

I had to restrain my impatience for some time, on account of Twenty Seven being reserved for a concluding effect. But, at last, we came to the door of his cell; and Mr. Creakle, looking through a little hole in it, reported to us, in a state of the greatest admiration, that he was reading a Hymn Book.

There was such a rush of heads immediately, to see Number Twenty Seven reading his Hymn Book, that the little hole was blocked up, six or seven heads deep. To remedy this inconvenience, and give us an opportunity of conversing with Twenty Seven in all his purity, Mr. Creakle directed the door of the cell to be unlocked, and Twenty Seven to be invited out into the passage. This was done; and whom should Traddles and I then behold, to our amazement, in this converted Number Twenty Seven, but Uriah Heep!

He knew us directly; and said, as he came out – with the old writhe, -

'How do you do, Mr. Copperfield? How do you do, Mr. Traddles?'

This recognition caused a general admiration in the party. I rather thought that everyone was struck by his not being proud, and taking notice of us.

'Well, Twenty Seven,' said Mr. Creakle, mournfully admiring him. 'How do you find yourself today?'

'I am very umble, sir!' replied Uriah Heep.

'You are always so, Twenty Seven,' said Mr. Creakle.

Here, another gentleman asked, with extreme anxiety: 'Are you quite comfortable?'

'Yes, I thank you, sir!' said Uriah Heep, looking in that direction. 'Far more comfortable here, than ever I was outside. I see my follies, now, sir. That's what makes me comfortable.'

Several gentlemen were much affected; and a third questioner, forcing himself to the front, inquired with extreme feeling: 'How do you find the beef?'

'Thank you, sir,' replied Uriah, glancing in the new direction of this voice, 'it was tougher yesterday than I could wish; but it's my duty to bear. I have committed follies, gentlemen,' said Uriah, looking round with a meek smile, 'and I ought to bear the consequences without repining.' A murmur, partly of gratification at Twenty Seven's celestial state of mind, and partly of indignation against the Contractor who had given him any cause of complaint (a note of which was immediately made by Mr. Creakle), having subsided, Twenty Seven stood in the midst of us, as if he felt himself the principal object of merit in a highly meritorious museum. That we, the neophytes, might have an excess of light shining upon us all at once, orders were given to let out Twenty Eight.

I had been so much astonished already, that I only felt a kind of resigned wonder when Mr. Littimer walked forth, reading a good book!

'Twenty Eight,' said a gentleman in spectacles, who had not yet spoken, 'you complained last week, my good fellow, of the cocoa. How has it been since?'

'I thank you, sir,' said Mr. Littimer, 'it has been better made. If I might take the liberty of saying so, sir, I don't think the milk which is boiled with it is quite genuine; but I am aware, sir, that there is a great adulteration of milk, in London, and that the article in a pure state is difficult to be obtained.'

A Stranger Calls To See Me

From Chapter LXIII: "A Visitor"

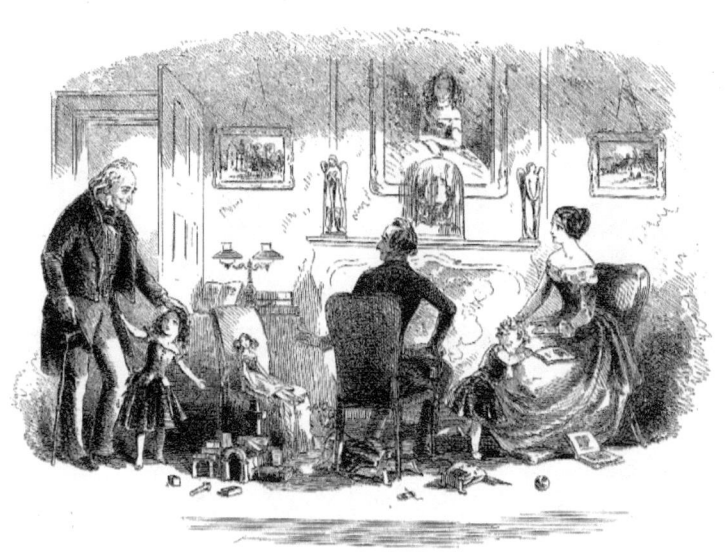

I had advanced in fame and fortune, my domestic joy was perfect, I had been married ten happy years. Agnes and I were sitting by the fire, in our house in London, one night in spring, and three of our children were playing in the room, when I was told that a stranger wished to see me.

He had been asked if he came on business, and had answered No; he had come for the pleasure of seeing me, and had come a long way. He was an old man, my servant said, and looked like a farmer.

As this sounded mysterious to the children, and moreover was like the beginning of a favourite story Agnes used to tell them, introductory to the arrival of a wicked old Fairy in a cloak who hated everybody, it produced some commotion. One of our boys laid his head in his mother's lap to be out of harm's way, and little Agnes (our eldest child) left her doll in a chair to represent her, and thrust out her little heap of golden curls from between the window-curtains, to see what happened next.

'Let him come in here!' said I.

There soon appeared, pausing in the dark doorway as he entered, a hale, grey-haired old man. Little Agnes, attracted by his looks, had run to bring him in, and I had not yet clearly seen his face, when my wife, starting up, cried out to me, in a pleased and agitated voice, that it was Mr. Peggotty!

It WAS Mr. Peggotty. An old man now, but in a ruddy, hearty, strong old age. When our first emotion was over, and he sat before the fire with the children on his knees, and the blaze shining on his face, he looked, to me, as vigorous and robust, withal as handsome, an old man, as ever I had seen.

'Mas'r Davy,' said he. And the old name in the old tone fell so naturally on my ear! 'Mas'r Davy, 'tis a joyful hour as I see *you, once more, 'long with your own trew wife!'*

'A joyful hour indeed, old friend!' cried I.

'And these heer pretty ones,' said Mr. Peggotty. 'To look at these heer flowers! Why, Mas'r Davy, you was but the heighth of the littlest of these, when I first see you! When Em'ly warn't no bigger, and our poor lad were BUT a lad!'

'Time has changed me more than it has changed you since then,' said I. 'But let these dear rogues go to bed; and as no house in England but this must hold you, tell me where to send for your luggage (is the old black bag among it, that went so far, I wonder!), and then, over a glass of Yarmouth grog, we will have the tidings of ten years!'

'Are you alone?' asked Agnes.

'Yes, ma'am,' he said, kissing her hand, 'quite alone.'

We sat him between us, not knowing how to give him welcome enough; and as I began to listen to his old familiar voice, I could have fancied he was still pursuing his long journey in search of his darling niece.

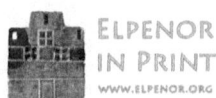

www.ingramcontent.com/pod-product-compliance
Lightning Source LLC
Chambersburg PA
CBHW020855180526
45163CB00007B/2518